Sally's and Nathan's voices are needed in this day and age of parenting. This book was an encouragement for me on so many levels, as a mama, friend, and woman in ministry. Both Sally and Nathan display the love and grace of Jesus toward each other, and that is a message that transfers to people all over the world.

JAMIE IVEY
Host of *The Happy Hour with Jamie Ivey* podcast

For anyone who has ever felt different, this inspiring book is a soothing balm and a call to arms to build the life of your dreams—no matter where you are.

CLAIRE DIAZ-ORTIZ
Author and entrepreneur, ClaireDiazOrtiz.com

I loved this book. Sally comes alongside parents raising difficult children and offers support, encouragement, and community. We get to see inside our kids through Nathan's words. It's a beautiful, deeply moving memoir that sends a clear and important message to our culture: Being different is more than okay. It's a gift.

KRISTEN WELCH
Author of *Raising Grateful Kids in an Entitled World*

I'm a mom with an outside-the-box kid—a child I love dearly but who brings me to my knees on a daily (sometimes hourly) basis. The wisdom from this book gives me the confidence and perspective I yearn for in parenting my quirky, beloved child. I'm beyond grateful that both Sally and Nathan have shared their story with us. It fills me with hope.

TSH OXENREIDER
Author of *At Home in the World* and *Notes from a Blue Bike*

I have watched the ministries of Sally and Nathan over the years, and I'm thrilled to see how God has used a "different" boy to bless so many. This is a book of hope and inspiration told through the eyes of a mom who, like so many parents today, must deal with the day-to-day challenges of working with a unique and special child.

DR. SCOTT TURANSKY
Cofounder of the National Center for Biblical Parenting; author of *Parenting Is Heart Work*

In *Different*, Sally Clarkson invited me to pursue God's heart for my own outside-the-box child. Her seasoned and experienced words lifted this mama's eyes off *What could be wrong with my child?* or *What could be wrong with me?* and on to Christ and all the possibilities of His beauty and power in the life of a person. This is a message for every parent's heart. I recommend these pages both to those who feel like they have outside-the-box children and to those whose children color within the lines.

SARA HAGERTY
Author of *Every Bitter Thing Is Sweet*

This is a story that will touch the heart of any mother. We bear the weight of our children's struggles, wishing we could take on their frustration and pain, often without help or answers. *Different* brings hope to every family with a child who breaks the mold. Sally and Nathan show us that God's strength is made perfect in weakness. Before He can use us greatly, He must wound us deeply.

AINSLEY ARMENT
Founder of Wild + Free

Reading *Different* lifted a huge burden off my chest, letting me breathe easy again. I can't thank Nathan and Sally enough for having the courage to share their story in detail. Just knowing there are other parents who have lovingly raised "different" kids gives me hope and helps me feel less alone as a mother.

JAMIE C. MARTIN
Editor of SimpleHomeschool.net; author of *Give Your Child the World*

God has used each of Sally Clarkson's books in a powerful way in my life as I travel down the ever-curving road of motherhood. I've loved them all, but *Different* is one of my new favorites. Sally's and Nathan's testimonies of God's faithfulness will increase your faith as you witness their doubt, heartbreak, and struggle, and as you come to see that you are not alone. Sally and Nathan speak right into your pain and uncertainty. In the rawness of each story, you will find strength, beauty, and hope.

ANGELA PERRITT
Founder and director of Love God Greatly; coauthor of *You Are Loved* and *You Are Forgiven*

For decades, Sally Clarkson has been a strong, wise guide for families. In *Different*, she is more vulnerable than ever before, recording a memoir of moving through a refining experience and sharing her notes from the journey. She and her son Nathan recount this ongoing struggle with faith-affirming honesty, offering insight and hope for families who face similarly bewildering battles. An at-times-painful story, *Different* is honest about Sally's and Nathan's progress without ending in a neat and tidy total victory. Instead, the book invites us into a faithful, resolved embrace of the story God is weaving even through the most painful and perplexing of our weaknesses.

S. D. SMITH
Author of *The Green Ember*; cofounder of www.storywarren.com

Sally and Nathan Clarkson's *Different* is a breath of fresh air for parents of different kids. While many books for outside-the-box kids focus on best practices, *Different* is . . . well . . . *different*. As you read the journey of this mother and son, you will smile, you will cry, and you will realize that you are *never* alone. And really, isn't that what we all want to know?

CAITLIN FITZPATRICK CURLEY
School psychologist, homeschooler, and founder of My-Little-Poppies.com

With this book, Sally Clarkson offers weary moms the nourishing feast for which they are starved. With equal parts empathy and wisdom, she breathes hope into the lives of parents who daily labor to lovingly raise outside-the-box children. Nathan grants us unprecedented, invaluable insight into the mind of the child as he grows. Sally assures us that though we will certainly be challenged, humbled, and humiliated, this story is not about us, but about being faithful to God to raise a uniquely challenged and challenging child. With warm understanding, she gives us tangible tools and healthy, hearty food for the journey.

ELIZABETH FOSS
Mother of nine; author of *Small Steps for Catholic Moms*

Sally and Nathan have given us hope by giving us the gift of sight. They have pulled back the curtain and helped us see the tender struggle of raising a child who breaks out of the boxes we try to fit people in. As a result, we learn to see challenge as a gift in disguise. This book makes visible what has been in plain sight to our family for years now: The Clarksons wholeheartedly love God and one another through the mess and the mystery of life and faith.

GLENN PACKIAM
Pastor; author of *Discover the Mystery of Faith*, *Lucky*, and *Secondhand Jesus*

Sally has protected her family by keeping certain stories hidden from the public sphere until now. The stories and truths in *Different* have not been shared before, and they will absolutely bring hope and freedom to those who struggle with their "different" children and think, *I can't do this; it's just too hard.* If you have an outside-the-box child, this is a must-read.

SARAH MAE
Coauthor with Sally Clarkson of *Desperate: Hope for the Mom Who Needs to Breathe*

As a parent who has often felt alone and completely out of my depth in raising a child who is outside the box, I found tender companionship in these pages. With vulnerability and candor, Sally and Nathan Clarkson have bravely lifted the veil on the struggles that are often unspoken and yet silently shape many families. Through this book, the journey of faith forged in their own lives has the power to breathe life into souls who are burned out on formulas and prescriptive solutions. If you are desperate for a way forward, longing for a future that is flourishing for your child, and dream of learning to parent with peace and grace, this book will guide you as it extends hope, healing, and the very present and tangible love of God for each of His children.

KRISTEN KILL
Author and blogger at *Hope with Feathers*

As a mother of two outside-the-box children, I found myself tearing up and nodding my head in agreement as I read *Different*. In the end, I felt so very grateful for this book. Sally and Nathan are both vulnerable and real as they describe the day-to-day life of a "different" child. Reading the unique perspectives of both mother and child is powerful. Moreover, the love that flows throughout this book makes even the most difficult experiences hope-filled and encouraging. I cannot recommend *Different* enough!

SHAWNA WINGERT
Author of *Everyday Autism* and *Special Education at Home*;
writer at www.nottheformerthings.com

different

The Story of an
Outside-the-Box Kid and
the Mom Who Loved Him

SALLY CLARKSON
NATHAN CLARKSON
ILLUSTRATIONS BY NATHAN CLARKSON

The nonfiction imprint of
Tyndale House Publishers, Inc.

Visit Tyndale online at www.tyndale.com.

Visit Tyndale Momentum online at www.tyndalemomentum.com.

Visit Sally Clarkson at www.SallyClarkson.com and www.MomHeart.com.

Visit Nathan Clarkson at NathanClarkson.me.

TYNDALE, Tyndale Momentum, and Tyndale's quill logo are registered trademarks of Tyndale House Publishers, Inc. The Tyndale Momentum logo is a trademark of Tyndale House Publishers, Inc. Tyndale Momentum is the nonfiction imprint of Tyndale House Publishers, Inc., Carol Stream, Illinois.

Different: The Story of an Outside-the-Box Kid and the Mom Who Loved Him

Designed by Nathan Clarkson and Dean H. Renninger

Edited by Anne Christian Buchanan

Unless otherwise indicated, all Scripture quotations are taken from the New American Standard Bible,® copyright © 1960, 1962, 1963, 1968, 1971, 1972, 1973, 1975, 1977, 1995 by The Lockman Foundation. Used by permission.

Scripture quotations marked NLT are taken from the *Holy Bible,* New Living Translation, copyright © 1996, 2004, 2015 by Tyndale House Foundation. Used by permission of Tyndale House Publishers, Inc., Carol Stream, Illinois 60188. All rights reserved.

Scripture quotations marked NIV are taken from the Holy Bible, *New International Version,*® *NIV.*® Copyright © 1973, 1978, 1984, 2011 by Biblica, Inc.® Used by permission. All rights reserved worldwide.

Scripture quotations marked NKJV are taken from the New King James Version,® copyright © 1982 by Thomas Nelson, Inc. Used by permission. All rights reserved.

For information about special discounts for bulk purchases, please contact Tyndale House Publishers at csresponse@tyndale.com or call 800-323-9400.

Library of Congress Cataloging-in-Publication Data
Names: Clarkson, Sally, author.
Title: Different : the story of an outside-the-box kid and the mom who loved him / Sally Clarkson and Nathan Clarkson.
Description: Carol Stream, IL : Tyndale House Publishers, Inc., 2016. | Includes bibliographical references.
Identifiers: LCCN 2016041361 | ISBN 9781496420114 (sc)
Subjects: LCSH: Parents of children with disabilities—Religious life. | Parenting—Religious aspects—Christianity. | Child rearing—Religious aspects—Christianity. | Clarkson, Nathan. | Clarkson, Sally. | Mothers and sons—Religious aspects—Christianity. | Obsessive-compulsive disorder in children—Patients. | Obsessive-compulsive disorder in children—Patients—Religious life.
Classification: LCC BV4596.P35 C53 2016 | DDC 248.8/431--dc23 LC record available at https://urldefense.proofpoint.com/v2/url?u=https-3A__lccn.loc.gov_2016041361&d=DQI FAg&c=6BNjZEuL_DAs869UxGis0g&r=ZlF6A1J_SMm9xAyjgyDor34CB-fqQRaraBLN VSdnrVo&m=2gKdDxMXrJhTp9UCpWHrrAWSFzF8P4dcYqsF6vggEJA&s=yGr4wilt8O WejcGQX5DAgRoolOAYdFx7blo6gEP6a-U&e=

Printed in the United States of America

22 21 20 19 18 17 16
7   6   5   4   3   2   1

To my loving mother, who was the first to show
me that being different is beautiful.

NATHAN

To my Nathan, whose full name means
"gift of God"—and so you truly are.

SALLY

CONTENTS

READ THIS FIRST
(EVEN IF YOU NEVER
READ INTRODUCTIONS)

NATHAN

They tell me "Stop." "Just don't." "Be normal."
So I try and I try and I try and I try
Not to let the demons in my mind
Be the ones who define
My every move,
My every thought,
My every rhyme.
But sometimes I feel like I'm all alone in a crowded room,
And no matter what I try, or what I do,
I can't make my eyes see like they're supposed to.
I can't see the world like the rest of you do
Because I've got something called OCD—
Obsessive-compulsive disorder—
But I'm starting to think these letters mean something
*   different,*

Less of a sitcom and more of a horror.
Maybe the O stands for "Oh, my God,
Why did you give this to me?
Why can't I just be normal like he or she?
Why can't I feel clean
And not feel the need to wash my hands until they bleed?"
Maybe the C stands for "C'mon, can't you see I'm in pain?
I can't even hug, kiss, or touch my loved ones
As they leave on a plane."
And maybe the D stands for "Despair,"
Like the kind that I felt when I sat on those stairs
With my head in my hands and I said, "This is not fair.
God, do you care?
God, can you tell that this man that you love is living
      in hell?"

And there in the silence I heard God say,
"My son, my son, I made you this way."

I said, "God, you've got to be kidding me! My mind is
      all wrong."
He said, "Son, don't you see your mind is a song?
It's a song I wrote for only you to sing.
It's unique and it's beautiful and it will help others see."

AS YOU READ MY STORY, IT IS MY HOPE THAT YOU MIGHT FEEL UNDERSTOOD AND KNOW YOU AREN'T ALONE ON THE JOURNEY OF BEING DIFFERENT.

I pressed Record on the camera staring at me atop the tripod, then quickly walked back to stand in front of my backdrop—a black sheet draped across my front door. I took a deep breath, locked eyes with the lens, and began.

I had the words typed out on my phone, but I didn't need to look at the screen. I knew them by heart because they had been swirling around in my head for the past month.

I've never really thought of myself as a poet. But for some reason, as I went to express my innermost thoughts, they came out in verse. Now here I was about to perform and upload a piece of spoken-word poetry that came directly from my heart for the world to see.[1]

For as long as I can remember, I wondered if I was the only one who felt this way—that it was me and then the rest of the world. So I decided to pour all the years of frustration, hurt, and wandering into a two-minute video and set it free into the world, hoping that maybe it would reach someone who felt the same. The poem offered no stats, quick fixes, or life hacks. It simply shared a glimpse of my story—all I really had to offer.

Little did I know when I hit Upload Video that in the next few days it would gain thousands of views. Then, as the views added up one by one, I started receiving messages and comments from viewers around the world.

"Thank you so much for this."

"This is my exact experience."

"I have always felt the same way."

"I've always felt different too."

It was amazing, beautiful, and humbling to know that a roughly made home video could connect and encourage people from every walk of life. People who had felt like me.

People who had always felt different.

These pages you have opened explore what it's like to grow up different. They are told from my point of view and also from my mother's, because this is a journey we've shared.

This book will not try to fix you. You won't find statistics or studies or a bunch of how-tos. Instead, we'll simply share our stories and our personal thoughts. We've also included a few of my drawings, which enabled me to tell my story and express my feelings in another way.

I feel confident with this approach because I have found that stories are powerful. They have the ability to reach out, inspire, and give us hope. It is my hope that with every page you turn, as I share my heart, you will perhaps find yourself thinking, *Me too*. That as you read a little more of my story and my mom's, you might feel understood—perhaps for the first time—and know you aren't alone on the journey of being different.

Sally

Tonight is the eve of my sixty-third birthday. Having stolen a few rare minutes alone on my front porch, I've been rocking gently in one of my white Cracker Barrel rocking chairs, sipping a cold drink, and listening to music as the fresh mountain breezes gently rattle the aspen trees in my yard.

I've also been reflecting on my life as Nathan's mother and wondering how to introduce you to my side of this story.

As I pondered these memories, music from one of my favorite film scores came floating from my tiny speaker—part of a playlist my musician son, Joel, recorded for me to listen to when I am relaxing. Cellist Yo-Yo Ma was playing a song from the 1986 movie *The Mission*. A hauntingly beautiful piece, the kind that wraps itself around your soul and touches deep, unspoken-of places inside that no one sees, it reflects both the exceptional beauty of the movie and the heartbreak found within the story. How well I remember that bittersweet story of a man trying to find redemption for his personal deficiencies and the mistakes he has made in the journey of his life.

As I listened to the countermelody of the cello mixed with the lighter refrain of the main tune, the sadness of the song brought tears to my eyes. Then I realized that this deeply beautiful music was a reflection to me of my son Nathan's story—profoundly rich, filled with vibrant and beautiful notes, but possessing a melancholy side as well.

This is our story, at once a tale of tears and heartbreak and a depiction of adventure, joy, and laughter and the unbreakable bond between mother and son. There's a lot about it that even today I don't understand. But this I know: God must have loved me a lot to give me the gift of Nathan.

The name means "gift of God." And Nathan *is* a gift—to me, to our entire family, and to many other people as well. But from the very beginning, Nathan was different from other children. He was my outside-the-box little boy, different in a very different way.

....

There is a memory from early in Nathan's childhood that is burnished deeply into my mind, the vividness of which has never gone away. Perhaps it was the defining moment when God spoke to my heart: *This child is truly a different kind of different. There is no formula, no disciplinary philosophy that is going to work with this little boy. This one will require blindly walking by faith, with a willingness to learn and understand how to be his parent. I made him. I will teach you. Are you willing to learn and grow?*

As a mama of three little ones under five years old, I lived in a tornado of activity. Someone was always talking, crying, making messes, needing me. But on this particular day, just rolling myself out of bed required all of my mental and physical strength. Exhaustion rolled over me like a fog, clouding my thoughts. Gathering suitcases, car seats, blankies, stuffed animals, and snacks, not to mention clothing three squirming bodies, required herculean strength.

By eight thirty that morning, I was already running on empty. The day already seemed a week long, and all we had done was to get up, eat breakfast, get dressed, grab our packed bags, and cram ourselves into our little car. But we had many more hours—and miles—to go. We were moving from California to Texas, a process that would take eighteen hours of plane trips and car rides. For me, the prospect presented a formidable challenge.

And then there was Nathan.

Already just beyond toddlerhood, Nathan was clearly different from other kids. Not different because of his face shape or his freckles or his personality. A different kind of different. He did not fit into any boxes we could define. Agitation seemed to be a part of his internal motor that revved up each day. People and the world at large seemed to bring him frustration on a regular basis. Every ordinary moment held the possibility of an explosion. How in the world would Nathan make it through two plane trips, three airports, and an entire day of interrupted routines without melting down?

He didn't. The day almost did me in.

Coping with a toddler who was wiggling, screaming, fussing, and resisting at every point of that journey left me deeply discouraged and emotionally flat. My husband, Clay, and I took "Nathan" turns through the plane rides, the long lines of waiting, the sitting still during the trip, the strolling around the airport as we waited for the next leg of the journey, leaving our two older—but not much older!—children to more or less fend for themselves.

Yes, I was "that mom"—the one with the squirming, screaming child that everyone points at and hopes they will not have to sit next to on the plane.

But finally we made it to our destination in Dallas. Surely reprieve would be ahead. And we would be stopping for food at one of Clay's favorite restaurant destinations. Located in a very ritzy and prominent part of town, this beloved establishment was patronized by the wealthy of the neighborhood. The bakery, established by a fine pastry chef, attracted hundreds of people each day. And the dinner buffet—an intriguing mixture of sophisticated dishes and comfort food—made this a special place to Clay. Assuming there would be something to please every palate, he hoped it would be a treat for the kids and me as well.

At the restaurant, we all made it through the buffet line. We intentionally picked a table in the far corner of the room, as far from the crowded center as possible. I had wrestled Nathan in my arms through the whole line and to our seats, hoping that food would appease him for just a few short minutes so I could gobble down my food.

But just as we all sat down at our table and began to eat, Nathan slid down from his chair to the floor, stretched out to his full little-boy length, and began to scream and yell and throw food. I tried to soothe him and placate him, but he lunged out to strike me.

That did it.

I got to my feet and walked away, leaving my toddler screaming and kicking on the floor. I hoped that somehow Clay and his mother, who had joined us, would find the heart to stay with him, because I couldn't. Exhausted and frazzled, having spent every ounce of patience I could muster, I could find nothing inside to deal with him at that moment. I was wasted from the embarrassment of everyone watching and whispering and pointing. After giving, loving, trying hour after hour (and day after day) to figure out something that would appease this little boy, I had reached what felt like the end of my rope.

And yes, I felt guilty. Guilty for leaving him, for leaving Clay and my mother-in-law to deal with him, definitely guilty for leaving his brother and sister quietly eating at the table and pretending they did not see what was going on. But at that moment I had no intention of going back. I had served, loved, held, comforted, run after, placated to the end of my strength. Somehow they would all have to cope without me.

I casually walked across the room to the bakery counter, where elegantly frosted cakes and delectable pies filled the racks. Though I was seething with frustration, I put on a calm front, studying the baked goods as if planning a purchase. It was my way of hiding from all the faces, the dirty looks, the insecurity I was feeling at that moment. Whisper-praying that I would be able to settle down, I tried to regain control over my raging emotions.

As I stood there, Nathan's screams still permeating the room, an elderly man who was attending to customers at the bakery display looked at me, not knowing I was the child's mother. "That boy needs a strong hand!" he said in a booming Texan drawl.

I shook my head in agreement, looking over at my family as if I didn't know them. But inside I was thinking, *I don't know what he needs, but he needs something I cannot give right now.*

The memory was a defining one for Clay and me. We already knew that something was different about Nathan. He had moments of sweet little-boy antics, but we never knew when he would erupt in frustration, anger, and agitation at a moment's notice—and we had no idea how to settle his little heart.

Of course, any little one might be frazzled by a day traveling across thousands of miles. But this extreme behavior was becoming more and more common to our daily family life. And this was the beginning of our trying to figure out what made him such an outside-the-box little boy and how we could possibly parent him.

It took a long time before we finally had names for some of Nathan's differences. Actually, what we eventually had were letters that described clinical disorders and a form of medically diagnosable mental illness:

- OCD—obsessive-compulsive disorder
- ADHD—attention-deficit/hyperactivity disorder
- ODD—oppositional defiant disorder

Added to this alphabet soup were some learning issues, some personality quirks, a strong will, plus a number of characteristics that have some qualities of autism and even now defy our understanding. And eventually we did find some help and support to add to the many things we learned through trial and error and love and listening—and lots and lots of grace.

We also learned, through the same trial and error and grace, to hold fast to what our hearts insisted (at least in quiet moments). That our boy was not a diagnosis. Not a problem to be solved or a disorder to be fixed. He was a child to be guided and trained and gloried in. And Nathan's differences—yes, even the ones that sometimes exasperated him and us—were, like Nathan himself, also part of the gift he is to the world and to us as his family.

Today Nathan is twenty-seven, and I can honestly say he is one of my closest, dearest friends. There is almost no one I would rather talk to, and few understand my dreams, thoughts, ideals, and struggles the way he does. I learn so much when we collaborate on projects together, as he is a constant source of ideas and mental stimulation for me. But as far as we know to this date, he will carry his issues with him his whole life, and we as a family will continue to learn more each year about how to love him better, how to adjust to his unique needs, and how to walk with him through his story more graciously.

Last fall, after he made his first movie, *Confessions of a Prodigal Son*, which was sold in Walmart and later picked up by Netflix, Nathan started receiving letters from all over the world.

"Mom," he told me, "most of the letters I get are from kids or parents wondering how I made it through childhood and lived to make a movie. We should write a book together, telling people our story—how we made it, how I felt, how you felt along the way. People like us need someone to identify with amidst their disabilities and differences."

"Are you sure you want me to be honest about how I felt along the way? Are you sure you don't mind people in the public arena knowing your story and struggles? If we write it, we will need to reveal some of the raw stories that took place in our family."

"I want it to be real. And I want to help people like us because we had so very few to encourage us along this path. I think we should do it, Mom."

And so, his idea became this book. We've written it as a team—in the hope that our experience might help those who struggle with being different and those who love them.

....

Before we go much further, it might be helpful for you to know a little bit about our journey as a family. Because this book is written thematically—the chapters and stories don't proceed in strict chronological order—you might find them easier to follow if you know a little more from the outset about who we are and where we've been.

We are a ministry/entrepreneur/artistic family. After becoming a woman of faith in college and working on college campuses for a couple of years, I embarked on my first missionary assignment—to Communist Poland—when I was just twenty-three. Clay and I were friends for many years, but we finally dated and got married when I was in my late twenties. We welcomed Sarah, our firstborn, while we were living in Denver, Colorado, and we had Joel two and a half years later in Vienna, Austria. Nathan arrived another two and a half years after that in Long Beach, California. And Joy, our beloved "caboose," would not come along until another six years later, when we lived in Texas.

Because of the pioneer nature of our work, we moved seventeen times when our first three children were little. For a time, when we were establishing our ministry and publishing enterprise (without a salary!), we lived with Clay's mother in tiny Walnut Springs, Texas—population 712! These were the wild years when our children roamed free on two hundred acres of land full of snakes, bugs, and fields to explore and adventures at every turn. It was here that Joy was born, a joyful surprise when I was just shy of forty-two. Next came a move to the Rocky Mountains, where our home backed up to twenty-five thousand acres of national forest. Finally, after one more move to Tennessee, we settled in our beloved home in Monument, Colorado, where we have lived for the past twelve years.

Through it all, Clay and I remained involved in our work and ministry. I wrote thirteen books. Clay added more. We traveled the world together, speaking at conferences and to a variety of audiences. Our children were raised by our sides as we worked from our home and spoke in hotels and conference centers, spending time with people from many different cultures and backgrounds. Home was always a haven we cherished between travel for ministry, but we also learned—and taught our children—to "make home" wherever we were.

Now, even though we have finally settled down, in a sense, we remain a traveling family. Clay travels less these days because of some back issues, but I am still the adventurer. Our work still takes me across the country and to many international venues, and I take advantage of any excuse to visit our children wherever they are in the world. As I write this, Sarah is married and living in Oxford, England, while completing her theology degree. Joel lives near her in Cambridge, pursuing a graduate degree in choral music, composition, and conducting at the university there. Joy is completing her master's at the University of St Andrews in Scotland. And Nathan, after studying acting in New York City and then pursuing his dreams in Los Angeles, is now back in New York, actively involved in a career as an actor, screenwriter, filmmaker, blogger, and author.

Nathan and I have always had a very close personal relationship. Most OCD kids, we have learned, have one parent who acts as the "confessor" in their lives—the one they go to daily to tell their recurring thoughts and find relief from the guilt those thoughts carry, the one with whom they find acceptance and a sense of safety. From the time Nathan was very little, I played this role in his life. I was also the parent who was most often home to deal with his issues on a daily basis and who researched possible diagnoses and treatments as we worked on understanding him through the years. Consequently, this story is focused on the two of us. Clay was closely involved, of course, as were the rest of our children, but what you will read here is mostly about mother and son and our journey together.

One more thing that might be helpful for you to know is that Nathan is not our only different child. Some of our other kids have struggled with health and mental-health issues, including OCD. But their stories are their own stories to tell—if they wish—and they are quite capable of telling them. They are not a focus in this book.

So those are the basic facts about us. But they are just the facts. They aren't the story. The purpose of this book is to tell you Nathan's story—and mine. It's the story of how the two of us learned to flourish amidst the glory and challenges of who he was made to be.

A brief note about terminology: In this book we use the word *normal* in the ordinary, colloquial sense. We are aware that this can be a loaded word for some people. But when Nathan was growing up, we were all acutely aware of how different he was from what most people called "normal." So we have chosen to use the word, without quotation marks, to describe people with more typical or usual behaviors and attitudes, keeping in mind that the line between different and normal can be a blurry one.

Being Nathan's mother taught me so much about what really matters in life. It taught me how to see people through a different lens, to appreciate and validate the variety and differences of people without casting judgment on the ways they differ from me. I grew to become a healthier person as I came to understand and practice living well with the miraculous gift of Nathan in my life.

But I confess that I often felt alone as I struggled through this journey. I didn't have much in the way of a support system. Rarely did I meet someone who had the time to empathize with my story or help me figure out my puzzle—even Clay did not fully comprehend Nathan's issues or diagnosis for many years—and often I did not have a clue how to access Nathan's bigger-than-life issues. And so much of the advice that was proffered to me was inadequate at best and insulting at worst.

Nathan grew up before support groups, testing, counseling, and help in these areas were as available as they are today. As a result, I often walked in darkness, depressive thoughts swirling deep inside as I struggled to find a way to reach my son and to accept and cope with both his limitations and my own.

This sense of being on my own, trying to figure out this walk through an unlit hallway, followed me through many years. And I have learned that this isn't unusual, even today. Many parents of different children journey through baffling days, months, and years before they discover and accurately diagnose their children's issues, so feeling alone and incompetent is typical. If that's where you find yourself, I hope that our story will help in some small measure. If you are raising a child who consistently pushes your buttons, whose behavior and motivations often baffle you, whose personality and emotional issues differ significantly from the norm, we hope you will find companionship and understanding here.

This is not really a how-to book, however; nor is it a "how to get it fixed" book. It does not delve into diagnostic issues, weigh the pros and cons of medications, or tell you what kind of counselors to seek—although I assure you we have run the gamut of input and considered every possible approach.

Some of what we learned is sprinkled through the book as part of our story. But this is not a medical treatise, and we are not writing to point you to one more formula, one more way of limiting what you eat, or one more set of natural products to "solve the problem." We are simply sharing what happened to us in hopes that it will help others who travel a similar road.

This journey has been a true adventure for Nathan and me. We faced challenge and danger, but we also encountered love and grace at every turn of the path. As in all the areas of our lives, we walked it hand in hand with God, asking for wisdom, seeking grace, and growing in understanding. He is the true hero of our story, and we pray you will find His companionship worthy of your trust in your own story. May the same also be true for those you love as you come to terms with what *different* means in your life.

If you have ever felt unaccepted for who you are, it is our hope that this book will help you feel validated, accepted, and affirmed for being unique, for having a distinctive life story.

If you live with a "different" person and share his or her struggle, we hope you will find strength, understanding, and perhaps some helpful strategies.

Whoever you are, we hope you will find grace for the ways you and those you love are different and outside the box.

In our story of hope, may you find hope for your own story as well.

I'm Different

Learning to See and Celebrate
God's Fingerprints in Our Lives

NATHAN

I've always known I was different. It wasn't something I chose or an identity I one day decided to wear. Being different is woven into the very fabric of who I am. Part of it comes from the various "disorders" that have challenged me and my family, and part of it simply comes from the outside-the-box personality God decided to give me.

Being different has made itself evident in every corner of my life, peeking out and reminding me whenever I start to think I might be normal.

I know I'm different because when other children were content with walking on the sidewalk, I felt the need to climb the rails. Because when others' questions would stop, mine seemed to go on without end, often frustrating those who ran out of answers.

I know I'm different because when I was fifteen I began taking six showers a day and washing my hands until they bled.

I know I'm different because my mind seems to change channels at will, making it nearly impossible to focus on any one thing for more than a few minutes.

I know I'm different because no matter how hard I looked at the math problem or how many times my tutor explained it, my mind simply couldn't grasp the simple numerical basics that seemed to come so easy to my friends and siblings.

I know I'm different because while I long for affection, I am often scared to touch the ones I love for fear of contaminating them.

I know I'm different because even now as a twenty-seven-year-old adult, there are times when the weight of the world seems so heavy I don't feel able to leave my apartment.

I know I'm different because I've been told so by every important person in my life.

Sally

"Do you just try to be different?" That was one of the most familiar phrases of my childhood and youth and even into my adulthood—though I was not consciously aware of this until I pondered my life while trying to figure out Nathan's.

The message wasn't *I love your uniqueness, your individualism.*

It was *Why can't you just fit in?*

"Since you are so pale and blond, you will have to try harder to have color in your face. You will need to wear mascara and lipstick every day to look beautiful."

"Are you watching your weight? And when was your last haircut?"

"That's a strange thing to say. Why would you even think that?"

"You try to think up every weird ideal and decision to pursue—just to embarrass our family."

These messages and others like them were the foundation of my psyche as a girl growing up. After I became an adult, the criticism was more often implied than spoken, but I heard it loud and clear: "Please don't tell my friends about the books you have written. Your values are a little bit 'out there,' and we wouldn't want to give anyone the wrong impression."

And the theme of all this communication was *You're different—and that's not okay.*

I was not *trying* to be different. I just was. I thought differently. I questioned things as they were. School bored me. I bounced my foot nervously during church and probably talked too much. I was definitely a little wild and dramatically idealistic in my values and dreams. And that made some of my family uncomfortable. They wanted me to fit in.

I realize now that I was probably one of those children

who today would be diagnosed with an alphabet's worth of letters—ADHD, OCD, perhaps a couple of other *D*s. Those terms are part of my daily vocabulary now, but that wasn't true back then. My parents certainly weren't informed of such things. There were fewer resources and less understanding of learning issues and mental illness. And of course I had no idea these issues framed my life. I only knew that I frustrated others from time to time by just being myself.

So I just muddled through. Because of training and peer pressure to conform, I managed (mostly) to hide my differences. Looking back through the corridors of my life, I now realize that I "stuffed" and suppressed my feelings and learned how to pull back so other people would accept me. I learned to avoid the conflict of being misunderstood *again*. Only much later, through time and experience and especially Nathan, would I come to a different understanding about being different.

I am writing this from the haven of my small, covered deck, sipping my cup of hot tea as I gaze out at tall pines swaying in the whispering wind. Yes, I'm out here again. Being outdoors is one of the best ways I know to find peace for my always active mind. And life is good, because finally I feel at ease in my own skin. I have come to actually like who I am, at least most of the time. But the journey of liking who I am, as I am, with all my strengths, passions, flaws, and imperfections, has been a long journey. It has taken most of my life.

I have always had secret dreams, pleasures, and ideas

bubbling inside me as well as an adventuresome spirit—a willingness to take risks, to experience life at its fullest, to question hypocrisy, and to point it out when others kept silent. All this plus a larger-than-life personality type meant I was often just too much for some of my family, though others in my world of friends loved the "bigness" of who I was.

My sweet mama, especially, struggled to cope with what I was like. She was a devoted and loving mama, but it took me years to understand that she was probably insecure and terrified that I might do something that would bring her criticism from her family or friends. *I* wasn't the one with a problem, in other words. *She* was. She had no idea how to accept me and to validate the person I was on a daily basis.

Let me add that I am long past blaming my parents and especially my mother. She did the best she could within the limits of her own perspective. She was a generous person, and she gave me a love for life in many areas where she felt comfortable. She also (inadvertently) taught me a valuable lesson that has served me well as a mama—that it is easy for parents to pass on unnecessary guilt, shame, and insecurity to their children because we fear the rejection of critical and judgmental people in our lives. So if I can help other parents understand the profound importance of accepting children as they are, perhaps I can save those children from some of the anguish I felt for many years.

There are an infinite number of ways to be different and to feel like one doesn't fit in. The difference can be personality driven. It can involve physiological issues, mental illness, or emotional issues, and can be shaped by experience. (Nathan's case, it turned out, did involve several clinical disorders as well as a number of personality quirks that set him apart from the crowd.) And feeling different—being different—is something our culture, especially our Christian culture, does not talk about much. People often turn their heads away from people and situations they don't understand and pretend they do not exist. And the words "mental illness" can make them positively squirm.

But the truth is, *all of us are a little bit quirky in some way or another.* All of us have Achilles' heels, uniquely vulnerable areas of our bodies, minds, and personalities. And some of us, to be honest, are a little quirkier than others—which is why we struggle so much and why other people—especially parents, teachers, and authority figures—have a hard time dealing with us. We are not convenient to their expectations of how life ought to play itself out.

But these personality differences, these outside-the-box preferences and approaches to life, don't have to be liabilities. Or they don't have to be *only* liabilities. They can actually be a gift to us and to others who are willing to look at life through our unique lenses.

Through my years I have discovered that most of us hide a great deal of who we are deep inside, fearing to reveal our flaws, our failures, our weaknesses, our wildness, and especially our "craziness," because we do not want to be rejected by others. Peer pressure and the voices of authority teach us that we should conform to the boxes of cultural expectations because it will save us from criticism.

Yet psychologists know that "stuffing" our real feelings and thoughts only produces havoc in our bodies, hearts, and minds. Learning to love ourselves, to be humble enough to admit our limitations, to truly appreciate the gifts our differences bring while also being willing to accept help and healing for the most painful ones, gives us greater mental, emotional, and spiritual health.

God made each of us with a unique set of "fingerprints"— our basic personality, physical makeup, and mental capacity, not to mention our God-given spirit. And we each face a unique set of life circumstances—health issues, teaching and modeling, experiences such as success and failure, nurture and abuse. All of these shape our unique story, which often defines our external behavior. But even in this broken world, where our differences often come with burdensome baggage, the imprint of God on our lives still gives value to each one of us as we are.

We are so often encouraged to fit into the boxes of academic achievement, intellectual prowess, recognizable achievements, personality profiles, status, money, power, external significance—to perform, to fit in the box, to be acceptable. Yet our wonderful God loves us unconditionally, now and forever. We do not have to work to please Him. He values us for what is inside our hearts—our character and integrity, our ability to love, to be faithful, to help others, and to show compassion. Our individual personalities are a gift of His design so that we might add color and variety to the world. And He can use our unique combination of circumstances—even the painful ones like mental illness—for our good and His glory.

Perhaps my own background of feeling inadequate for being "me" prepared me, at least a little, for the gift of my own outside-the-box boy, Nathan. Because I always wanted someone to know me and still love me—to actually *like* me as I was—I was predisposed to champion him with all of his differences.

But that doesn't mean it was easy! Far from it.

In fact, God must have a sense of humor because he gave me the gift of a little boy who was *really* different. A boy whose outsized needs and over-the-top behavior would test the far limits of my love, challenge my desire to have a heart of compassion, force my ability to live slowly and patiently, and defy my ability to tame or control my circumstances.

Nathan's differences stretched me and challenged my own limits of wanting to fit in, to not bring more criticism and judgment, and my deep desire to have life be controllable. By loving him through the peaks and valleys of his own life journey in our home, I learned even more the meaning of the preciousness and value of each human being, who is crafted mysteriously by the hands of God. I learned to appreciate and celebrate difference (not just "cope with it") because all human beings are a work of the Artist and have infinite value to the One who made them.

CHAPTER 2

I Run to You

·······································

Lessons from the Middle of the Night

NATHAN

The warm September air sat heavy on my face as I lay there in the dark room. Silence had fallen gently from the endless Texas sky onto our humble ranch house set picturesquely in the middle of Nowhere Town—Walnut Springs. The noise of talking and laughter, the noise of a fully lived-in home, had faded into echoes, and the world had quietly gone to sleep. But I was wide awake, staring into the dark, unable to take part in the rest my family had found.

Just an hour before, as night had begun to creep in from outside, my two siblings and I had been gently ushered to bed with a pat from Dad and a good-night kiss from Mom, followed by a rehearsed prayer my mother recited over us each night:

"The Lord bless you and keep you. The Lord make His face to shine upon you . . ."

Her words still hung in the air as I lay there, tossing restlessly.

And I needed to hear them again.

You see, to my six-year-old OCD heart, that blessing had become much more than a simple nighttime routine. Slowly but surely it had grown into a ritual I depended on to find the peace to fall asleep. It was my assurance that it was okay to close my eyes and leave the day behind, the comfort I needed to feel all was right with the world.

I tried to make myself go to sleep, to force my body and mind into willful compliance, but to no avail. This was my nightly battle.

My eyes stayed wide open, my mind at attention, telling me over and over again that I needed one more blessing for everything to be all right. I knew in my head that one good-night prayer was enough. But I couldn't shake the nagging sense from deep within my brain that another prayer was needed if I was to find any peace that night.

This anxiety was no new sensation for me. As long as I could remember, my mind and I had been at odds, constantly battling for control of my thoughts. And as long as I could remember, it seemed, my mind had been winning. (I did not understand then, as I would later, that my OCD prompted a deep compulsion for rituals to be repeated over and over again in order to get centered.)

It's not that I didn't want to be normal. In fact, I earnestly desired to be like other people, whose thoughts were just that—thoughts. But for me at six years old, that seemed impossible—a battle too great for me to fight alone.

I restlessly turned over, and my eyes fell upon a figure gently breathing in and out, unaware of the battle taking place in my bed. My brother, Joel, was peacefully asleep like I should be, like the rest of the world was. I felt like sleep was a club I wasn't invited to. Like I was the only person alive, awake. Alone.

I watched my brother as he slept—no worries, no intruding thoughts, just rest. And I wondered if that was what it was like to be normal.

Would I ever be normal?

My eyes darted to the neon-red number that said 12:07. It was past midnight. I knew my options were disappearing with every second that ticked into the night.

Some nights were easier than others. Some nights I could ignore the voices long enough to fall asleep. But not tonight. They were simply too loud. Finally, in an act of desperation I flung my covers off, climbed out of bed, and walked resolutely toward the doorway of my room.

"Where are you going?" a voice said from behind me.

I stopped and turned to see Joel sitting up, rubbing his eyes. Like a thief caught red-handed, I froze, then replied.

"I need Mom."

Joel lay back down and effortlessly drifted back to sleep. I continued my mission—down the stairs and through the dark halls to my parents' bedroom.

I had hoped they'd still be awake. But as I walked in, my heart sank to find them both fast asleep. I paused, planning my next move. I took a breath and mustered as much courage as I could to walk to my mother's bedside and gently touch her shoulder.

Her eyes slowly opened.

"Nathan?" she said, half-surprised to see me, half already knowing why I was there.

"I can't get to sleep," I said in a whisper.

"Why not?" she replied.

"I need another prayer."

There was a heavy silence. My heart beat anxiously as I awaited her response, hoping I hadn't pushed my luck too far this time. This wasn't the first time I had found myself here at the edge of my mother's bed, asking for another bedtime blessing.

I wasn't trying to be bad. I wasn't trying to be selfish or disturb anyone. I simply didn't know how to approach this battle alone, so I had sought out the only one I knew who could make it right.

With a deep sigh, my mother finally pushed back her covers and climbed out of bed. She gently put her hand on my back and led me back down the dark halls, back up the stairs to my room, and back into my bed, where she pulled the covers up to my neck.

She put her hand on my forehead and gently brushed my hair to the side, tenderly kissed me, and spoke the words again.

....

Twenty years later and fifteen hundred miles away, in a studio apartment somewhere on the West Side of New York City, I lay on a mattress on the floor, looking directly up into the dark that had fallen over the metropolis that "never sleeps." I had just moved across the country and into a tiny room I now called home. It had been a long day in a new place, filled with all sorts of new problems to solve, and all I wanted to do was close my eyes and leave the day behind. But I couldn't. Something wasn't quite right, and no matter how much I wanted to sleep, I simply wasn't able to.

With every attempt to force myself under, my OCD came crashing through the roof of my mind, yelling at me again and again that things weren't okay and that they wouldn't be until I washed my hands and took another shower.

I knew in my head that I was clean. I knew cognitively that if I just shut my eyes, the world wouldn't come to an end. But like a dripping faucet in my brain, the unwanted and unwelcome thoughts continued.

At that point, my options were few. I could try to ignore the nagging and let it harass me until morning. Or I could spend the next thirty minutes wasting my time and energy on pointless rituals when all I wanted was rest.

I felt helpless, angry, and alone. I was ashamed that at

twenty-six years old I was still fighting the same battle as I was when I was six.

As I lay there, I thought back twenty years to the times like this when my mind was simply too much for me to handle. What a comfort it had been to have the loving arms of a parent to run to in the midst of my struggle. But I was all alone in a big city, feeling small. I didn't have my mother's prayer to tuck me in or my parents' consistent presence to calm my anxious heart.

Tears spilled out of the corners of my eyes. Then I was overcome with shame that as a fully grown man I could become upset to the point of tears over something as minuscule as "feeling dirty." I wanted to get out of bed and run to my parents' room to be met by a warm embrace and an understanding voice that would say, "It's okay. Everything's going to be all right, Nathan." But that wasn't an option this night.

Or was it?

I blinked my eyes in the dark and suddenly remembered the words my mother had spoken to me so many years ago, *I will always love you, and God will always be with you.* Suddenly, there in the dark, I remembered I wasn't alone. And while there was nothing I could do to make everything all right, there was Someone I could talk to. Someone who would share this dark night with me.

So with nowhere else to turn, I turned my gaze up and into the black, to the only parent I had available. I let my gentle and broken voice pierce the palpable dark: "I need Your help."

WHAT WE DO WITH LIFE'S DARK MOMENTS
DETERMINES WHO WE WILL BE.

I want to say that after talking to God that night, everything was immediately all right, that my OCD-induced anxiety disappeared and I never had another restless night. Unfortunately, that's simply not how life works.

We all live in a broken world full of dark nights. But what we do with those dark moments determines who we will be.

As a young boy my struggles led me to the presence of my loving parents. And now that I am a man, I am learning to let my struggles lead me to the presence of my loving heavenly Parent.

Sally

Exhaustion drugged me into unconsciousness every night when my children were little. I was chronically sleep deprived from year upon year of living with ear-infected, asthmatic, chronically ill children. By the time Nathan was born, I had learned, by sheer force of will, to place one foot in front of the other even when my eyes could barely stay open.

But Nathan was something else again.

Just as I would begin sawing logs, grasping at a few minutes of reprieve, desperately breathing the oxygen of rest into my depleted body, I would feel a tap, tap, tap on my shoulder from somewhere out beyond dreamland. And nightly I would slowly come to reality. *Oh, it's Nathan . . . again!*

This little blueberry-eyed, freckle-faced, giggling ball of constant energy pushed me to the limit all day long and all night long. Great love, true enjoyment, and lots of extroverted fun filled my days, but the exhausting parts were also a reality. There were delights and depletions—and a complex little boy who seemed to defy my efforts to understand him.

Nathan did not sleep through the night until he was four. And even then, he could not go to sleep without the repetitive assurance of my praying for him—even if I had prayed five minutes before and five times before that.

We resorted to every possible kind of strategy to change this frustrating bedtime pattern. Nothing worked. Harsh admonitions, strong requirements, regular patient assurance did not work. Ignoring him and pretending to be asleep did not work. Teaching him self-soothing techniques did not work. We repeated to ourselves all the advice that others gave us. *He is controlling you. You need to be firm and not give it to him.*

It didn't work.

Then I finally got it through my heart that Nathan couldn't help it. He really could not settle without *one more prayer.* That realization changed my entire approach.

I remember nights when my asthma flared up as a child. My mama would lie in bed close to me, singing, as I gasped for breath. I felt wrapped in her compassion for my struggling, frail body.

Couldn't I muster the same compassion for my own hurting child?

Investing in his heart really required so little of me, just a little more energy given late at night, but it meant the world to him. And practically speaking, attending to Nathan cost so much less than listening to him wail for hours, which would always awaken the others and leave us with an emotionally fraught sense of failure and anger for his not complying with our expectations that "children should be able to go to sleep with reasonable ease."

What I did instead was to quietly come to his bed, hold his soft little hand gently, and make him look into my eyes. "Now listen to me and pay attention, because this is a special blessing and I want it to go into your heart!" Then I would keep my voice as low and gentle as I could as I spoke:

"God bless my Nathan and help him to have a peaceful sleep. . . . Good night, my Nathan bug! Mama loves you. And now you can go to sleep, because we have tied all of the minutes of the day together, and you can leave them in God's hands."

Maybe it was these nightly blessing-prayers through all the years that God was listening to as He shaped Nathan day by day into a compassionate, humble, gentle man of moral and spiritual strength. I know they made a difference to me. My child heart reaching out to the loving heavenly Father gave me the strength I needed to make it through one more late night. Then another . . .

So that became our nightly routine year after year. Again and again.

Just as it had been from the beginning. Because Nathan and sleep had never peacefully coexisted.

Even just days after bringing Nathan home from the hospital, I'd begun to understand that my life was changing drastically. Month by weary month marched by as I tried to find the right formula to help my newest little boy settle down and rest.

The regular breathing of toddler Joel and almost-five-year-old Sarah gave rhythm to the darkness surrounding me as I attempted to comfort my restless infant in the darkness of the kids' room. After an hour and a half of holding him close to me and singing soft lullabies, his fourteen-pound body seemed a weight beyond reason.

I had changed his diaper to be sure he was dry, offered him water, tried song after song. Nathan still arched his little back and screamed and wailed beyond control. Nothing would comfort him. Not even exhaustion would bring him sleep.

I prayed so many desperate whisper-prayers during those nights when Nathan was little: "Please, God, please let him fall asleep. I am not sure I can keep going. Please calm him."

Still he screamed and writhed.

Clay took his turns walking the floor and singing, sometimes driving around in the night with Nathan cuddled in his car seat.

Same results.

As a mama of two other children, I knew this was not normal. Something was wrong. Nathan just would not calm. He would not easily go to sleep. Not if I left him in the crib. Not if I sang to him or talked to him. Not if I did all the myriad things that had brought soothing, peaceful sleep to my other two.

Dark desperation would float around my whole being

as I persisted to try to find a solution to "make" him stop screaming. But most nights and most days, Nathan remained a mystery.

A bleary-eyed, sleep-deprived mystery—to us and to our pediatrician, too.

Other Nathan mysteries filled our daytime hours as Nathan grew. Sometimes he was a sweet, happy, exuberant little boy, a total charmer. Other times, for no apparent reason, he would lie on the floor, scream and yell, and beg me to help with frantic eyes piercing my own. And often, no matter what I did, the agitation persisted.

Helpless and dead in my tracks, I did not know what to do. Feelings of despair and overwhelming frustration threatened me as I tried to reach this baffling little boy. Often I felt too tired to battle once more, only to be rebuffed.

Months passed. Years passed. Nathan remained an exhausting mystery.

How could I forget all the well-meaning, useless advice I received from so many friends intent on helping me control his unacceptable behavior.

"You just need to discipline him more."

"You are being way too lenient and not showing him who is the boss."

"You are raising a spoiled little boy."

"If you take away all of his sugar, he will be just fine."

"Have you tried essential oils?"

"Computer games that reprogram his brain?"

Or, or, or . . .

So many offered a guaranteed remedy they were certain would relieve Nathan of his troubles. I tried quite a few. Nothing worked.

My insecurity over my "failure" with this little one caused me at times to consider these friends' advice. I tried being stricter. I adjusted our diets. I sprang for the oils.

None of it worked.

But gradually, after years of praying and listening to my own heart, I observed some things about Nathan that helped me. I noticed he had a sweet heart and did respond to gentleness when I offered it to him. And he seemed to respond to touch; if I scratched his back while talking to him, he seemed to be able to listen better, to focus more. If I stayed right by his side during our homeschooling lessons and gave him all of my time and attention, he had a better chance of grasping new concepts. Patience and focused attention would often help him to respond and talk to me about what he was feeling. I prayed, pondered, and sought wisdom and education to find a way to reach him in the impossible moments, which still happened so very often.

No parenting book even got close to giving me insight. Most were formulaic, and many were harsh. "Just discipline him more, be firmer, show him who is boss." I already knew better than that.

Sometimes, I admit, I ignored my own instincts and observations out of my desire to have a more typical child and to avoid the stress and inconvenience of figuring out this demanding one. But voices inside me warned that this was going to be a very long, physically and emotionally demanding journey. I simply had to tame my own impatience to make it through with as much grace as I could muster.

Questions mounted:

- When was it right to hold firm and discipline Nathan?
- When did I need to respond to his meltdowns with grace and a blind eye?
- How would his behavior and my inability to control it affect the other children?
- What were the deep, unexpressed needs that drove him to act the way he did? And how could I learn how to meet those needs?
- How could I find grace for all the times I failed to connect to him?
- And what in the world was God thinking—entrusting me with this child I couldn't understand and failed so often?

Often I would rail against heaven and plead with God, asking Him all these questions and more in the dark, by myself.

One day, as the sun sank behind the mountain next to our house and the shadows deepened, I retreated to my bedroom for a cup of tea and a moment of quiet. As I sipped the last strong drops, I felt God whisper gently to my heart.

This is not a sprint. This is a long-distance marathon. Nathan can grow stronger over time and mature, but you need to leave him in My hands. You cannot figure it all out. But you can love him. I trusted you with him because I believed you would choose to do this. I hoped you would see inside his heart to draw out his dreams, to see what he felt. I hoped you would try to understand how his brain works. Every day you trust him to Me is a day I am honored by your faith. Tending Nathan faithfully when no one sees is a way you worship and honor Me.

If you accept this child as a gift from Me, I will use him as a blessing in your life. Let go of your questions, fears, and guilt. If you submit to My will with a humble heart, I will carry this burden for you so you can find peace.

A sense of freedom filled my heart when I understood that I didn't have to solve all our problems at once or even understand them. God would be with me every step of the way. He would fill in the holes of my inadequacy with His grace. And He was inviting me to a commitment of unconditional acceptance.

What I finally understood in that moment was that exemplary behavior was not God's main concern about me or Nathan—or with any of my children, for that matter. Our heavenly Father cared far more about developing hearts of love and obedience than He did about perfect performance. My reputation as a parent was safe with God even when my children threw tantrums, displayed immaturity, or engaged in outside-the-box behavior. And God really did care about my sacrament of praise to Him in the small moments when no one but He saw. When I kissed Nathan to give rest to his agitated heart every night, I was kissing the cheek of God.

When I gave Nathan a back rub or read him one more story, I was engaging in worship.

That changed perspective helped me see Nathan anew, as someone who needed to be understood, loved, and affirmed for his unique personality, dreams, and hopes. I was impressed to believe that no matter how he acted, no matter how he responded or didn't respond, he basically needed what all of my children, my husband, and even I needed—unconditional love, patience, a trusting friendship, and respect for who he was. He also needed character training, inspiration for his little-boy heart, exposure to Scripture to learn about his God, and consistent, persistent teaching that didn't demand set outcomes.

And I could give him all that because I was already doing it with my other kids—his gang, his "pack." I could be a cheerleader and believe forward into the man he would become.

I just couldn't control him.

And although Nathan needed much of what I was already doing with my other little ones, he also needed a different approach. I had slowly learned how to embrace, train, and lead my other little ones to respond to my mama love. But the same things I practiced with them did not always seem to work with Nathan.

So I had to change my expectations. He was, even more, my "by faith" child.

I don't understand you, but by faith I will trust that God understands you and that He will reach you.

By faith I will make it through one more baffling, frustrating day with you and seek to grow in patience.

By faith I will focus on your victories and not always harp on what you cannot do or control.

By faith I will trust that I will make it through all of your years at home and that God will help you grow into a man who honors Him.

By faith I will believe that all of the training, correcting, loving, helping is going into a foundational place in your heart, even though you don't show signs of responding at this moment.

By faith I will trust that all our struggles will be used for our good and not for evil.

By faith I will learn to see you as the blessing you are.

As I learned to accept Nathan uniquely for who he was, I began to learn that his capacity for self-control was different from that of the other kids. He simply did not have the same ability to respond to the reasonable requests I made to the other two. And when Joy was added to our gang, she eventually grew beyond Nathan in some areas (such as spelling and the ability to sit still and work), even though she was six years younger.

I knew beyond a doubt that I needed to understand Nathan's difficulties and help him interpret them in a way that would not crush his spirit. And gradually, over time, we made progress.

Through the seasons, I began to realize that as Nathan came to me and found me safe and trustworthy, a champion for his fraught little life, I was setting a pattern for him for how he would eventually learn to come to God. When I was gentle, kind, and patient, Nathan could believe that God was also gentle, kind, and patient. And eventually, slowly, he would learn that even when he was alone—even as an adult in a big city far from home—God would be there, waiting to help him through one more night.

Something else happened as I continued in faith, learning about Nathan, accepting him, practicing patience. A fresh, overwhelming love for this "wild one" began to bubble up in my heart. He was a generous gift to me. I could enjoy his antics and understand the person he was within. Compassion and sympathy won many days. And as I grew in this profound love for my boy, I began to see growth in my belief that God loved me even more profoundly. In loving Nathan, I was beginning to learn and feel the unconditional love I had always longed for.

Never would I want to leave the impression that I did not struggle with all the attention and time Nathan required of me every day. Nathan constantly disrupted my plans and challenged my control of life on a daily basis. And believe me, I often felt—and sometimes acted—challenged!

I am not a naturally selfless woman, nor a patient one. I'm the type to fly through life so that I can get a lot done—now! I usually have a strong sense of the way life should be, and I tend to get irritated when someone gets in my way or I can't make things "right."

But none of these qualities were practical or effective in responding to this one who needed my slowness and my attention in the midst of my busyness. And I had made a commitment to God to begin to see Nathan as a blessing. So slowly, slowly, as I relied on Him, I began to change. My capacity for patience increased. My ability to overlook Nathan's outbursts grew. And I began to deeply perceive that people made in God's image, no matter how challenging, are of more importance to Him than efficiency, control, or order.

Gradually I learned to leave my need for control and correctness behind. What did it hurt me to simply absorb his agitation instead of trying to change it all the time? I could choose to be the mature one in the daily confrontations and overlook a moment of his immaturity. I realized that correcting everything he did wrong and getting upset about it was not productive for me, for Nathan, or for our whole family. So instead of worrying about what others thought or about what I thought children should be like, I tried my best to focus on Nathan's true needs, his actual capabilities, and what he needed most to learn.

I aimed at reaching his heart through consistent instruction, encouragement, accountability, and training, moving him little by little toward self-control and responsiveness to our family ways. Choosing to live into my God-ordained role to shepherd this little boy through life took precedence over my need to be approved as a mother—and this release of expectations brought freedom and grace.

I also began to learn to speak forward to Nathan about his life. "I believe you will be a strong man someday. When you choose to make good decisions, you are growing stronger inside. I believe God will use you to help others, to write a great story with your life. I can't wait to see what you become. I believe in the great person you are going to become, and I love being your mama."

Gradually, as I persevered in these practices, I began to understand more what Jesus meant when He said, "Greater love has no one than this, that one lay down his life for his friends" (John 15:13)—when He sacrificed His own life for us, His unruly, selfish, outside-the-box children. As I made the choice over and over again to lay down my own life—by getting out of bed to comfort my little boy, by overlooking immaturity and seeking to train him in strength and self-discipline one day at a time, by cleaning spill after spill and settling argument after argument—I began to love Jesus more and appreciate His sacrificial love for me.

CHAPTER 3

Launch Code

···

The Beauty and Challenge
of Growing Up Different

NATHAN

I wiped the wet paint from my hands and stared up at the work in front of me.

It was almost finished.

I picked up a brush and drew in my breath, ready to make the finishing touches. I carefully applied strokes of black, blue, purple, and white for the stars. Then I took a step back and gazed at my handiwork—a mural of a home next to the sea, perched under a tree beneath a sky full of stars. I had copied it from my favorite CD cover, *The Everglow* by the band Mae,[2] and now it drew itself grandly across my bedroom wall and across the ceiling.

This was the final touch to my new room in the basement of our brand-new home. I had worked for hours toward the vision in my mind I longed to bring to life, and now it was almost done.

Since I was born, my family had packed up and moved every couple of years, never finding ourselves fully settled anywhere. But now we had finally decided to settle in Colorado. So for the first time in my fifteen years I had my own permanent domain I could make all mine.

I tossed my hair out of my eyes and looked at the walls surrounding me. Soon, I was sure, this room would be swirling with memories.

To my left was a full-length mirror. I would spend hours in front of it self-evaluating, practicing dance moves and flexing poses, and rocking out to the invisible crowds.

To my right you would see a shelf inhabited by a hundred plastic soldiers guarding the bed beneath two giant posters of Superman watching over me as I slept each night. These were friends who had accompanied me for years, inspiring me to be strong and brave.

And now, in front of me, lived the art I had brought to life. A picture of home. It was exactly what I wanted for my room.

The only problem was I hadn't exactly told my parents what I was up to.

Too excited about what I was doing to hear a no, I had decided (as usual) that it was "better to ask forgiveness than permission." So there was a twinge of nervousness as I called up the stairs.

"Mom, come here! I want to show you something."

"Be right there," she replied.

I waited anxiously, suddenly realizing that covering multiple walls and a ceiling with unapproved graffiti might not have been the best idea. But it was too late now. My adolescent passion had gotten me this far. I would have to ride it out.

I heard a knock at the door. I opened it slowly. My mother immediately spotted the changes.

She stepped inside, silently turning her head, taking the whole effect of the room in.

I bit my lip, dying to know my fate.

"What do you think?" I asked with trepidation.

"Nathan, it's beautiful. Exquisite!"

Suddenly my heart was put at rest. She liked it! She had seen the passion I had poured into it. Instead of being angry that I had (once again) wandered out of the lines of what was expected, she appreciated it because she loved who I was.

"Watch this," I said.

I stepped to the light switch and shut off the lights, revealing the hundreds of glow-in-the-dark stars I had painstakingly placed across the ceiling. The constellations of my creation brightened as our eyes adjusted in the dark.

My mom silently took it all in, admiring the effort I had put into my domain.

"Oh, Nathan, it's so you."

It wasn't what she had expected. It certainly wasn't what was typical. But she was right—it *was* me. That room didn't look like any other. It wasn't supposed to look like any other.

THE THINGS THAT MAKE US DIFFERENT CAN
BE THE THINGS THAT MAKE US STRONG.

It was simply supposed to reflect the passion of its designer—me. My mom saw that. And instead of expecting me to conform, she reveled in my uniqueness.

There's an idea that different is wrong, that being different is bad.

People who are different stick out. They don't fit into the usual way of doing things. They can be disruptive and difficult to deal with—even difficult for themselves to deal with. And while I know all too well that this is true, I'd like to come to the defense of different.

There's an idea that some people are normal and some are different.

Perhaps as you read these words you will think of someone you know, maybe someone you love, who fits the characteristics of being different. But maybe, just maybe, there have been times in your own life when *you* felt that no matter how hard you tried, you simply couldn't see life like "everyone else." Times when you've felt the whole world turn against you. Times when no matter how hard loved ones tried, they simply couldn't understand what you were going through.

Times when you yourself have felt different.

Now, your "different" may not be as obvious as mine is when I bounce off the walls with ADHD or wash my hands after touching food because of my OCD. But we all have things that make us unique. Different.

And I don't believe these are things to run away from or destroy—because the things that make us different can be the things that make us strong.

All too often, in a culture that demands conformity, we try to suppress the traits that just don't fit in, when in reality the things that make us different can be the things that make us beautiful, and are the traits that God wants to use in our lives to bring strength to others and reflect His beauty.

Most of my life I have been told to sit down, be good, and conform.

I have been asked, forced, and pushed into boxes I was never created to be inside of. Then I felt like a failure when I didn't fit.

I was also blessed to be born into a family that didn't want to squish me into a box, but instead pushed me to be the shape that God had designed me to be, no matter how different it looked or felt.

The truth is, we all are different in one way or another. The walls of each of our souls are covered with their own unique murals, and when God steps inside, He's not looking to change, whitewash, or push us to conform. Instead, He revels at the uniqueness He created each of us to have.

Sally

By the time fifteen-year-old Nathan presented me with his "big surprise," Clay and I had learned much about the fact that we would never be "in control" of our children, especially him. To this day, we never know what a day will hold with Nathan. But when he was a teen, his differences made ordinary teen issues bigger than they had ever been with our first two children.

Fortunately, by this time I had been stretched, challenged, humbled, and humiliated enough to know his story was not about me, but about being faithful to the God who had entrusted him to us.

It was when Nathan was a teen that we finally put names to some of his differences. He was diagnosed as having severe clinical OCD, which manifested itself as fifteen face washes (in the bathroom right outside our bedroom!) every night before he went to bed, multiple showers a day, food he couldn't eat, and food he didn't want *us* to eat or even touch (bacon, for instance). We were finding every day that there were new areas for us to "contaminate his life" just by being in his living space. And these incidents kept us constantly feeling that we were missing cues we'd never been given.

Nathan's additional ODD diagnosis helped explain his loud, argumentative personality, which constantly presented new areas of conflict. Because Nathan is quite intelligent, he could beat down any opinion—as long as he did not have to spell the words or write them out with correct grammar—and he never backed down from an issue he cared about. Dinner-table discussions often evolved into arguments, even as I sought nightly to create an atmosphere of harmony.

Yet this was the platform of life where we chose to engage with all the kids, discussing world issues, Scripture, convictions, stories, what they had learned that day. So all of us stretched and wiggled through the conflicts to enjoy our times together, knowing that the arguments were an inevitable part of our daily lives.

For me, weariness was a familiar companion as I tried again and again to move in the direction of a peaceful dinner. And yet those dinners together were foundational to all of us, an anchor in our day. (Now, as a grown man, Nathan counts these evenings among his fondest memories. He cherishes those times when deep friendship and fellowship was served each night with food as the medium for growth.)

All of these issues were in place long before Nathan was a teen, but adolescent hormones seemed to exaggerate them. It was almost as if they were on steroids! Anger quickly escalated to yelling. Frustration showed itself through tears. Passion to be "God's man" was a dramatically serious commitment. A deep (and natural) desire to fit in and to be approved by peers sent him on a careening search for acceptance and validation of his bigger-than-life self. And foolishness abounded with his immaturity and the quirks of his less-than-rational mind to deal with it all.

For example, after sixty-five hours of driving with me, Nathan got his driver's license, and I supposed he could handle driving himself to his local classes and back home. Yet within weeks of our giving him an old dark-green second-hand coupe, complete with black leather seats, he had totaled his new car.

"I know how to drive. It comes to me intuitively. Watch this!" he had announced to Joel as they skidded down a snowy street. "I don't need you to tell me what to do," he added when his brother warned of a looming stop sign. So he sped down our little street, found himself unable to stop at the corner, and slid into an oncoming car. A big lesson for him to learn, but one with consequences for me, because now I had to drive him to all of his activities again!

Over a course of eighteen months, Nathan earned six speeding tickets. Accompanying him to the local court to get his ticket reduced became old hat. And there were more incidents that shall remain our own private stories.

All of this might come as a surprise to those who have followed our ministry through the years. But even though our lives were quite public and our audience often examined anything they could find out about us, we always sought to give our children, including Nathan, as much privacy as possible. We wanted them to have room to grow. Writing this book now and revealing so much about our crazy life together was Nathan's choice.

And yes, life was a little crazy for the Clarkson family in the years when Nathan was a teen. But in the midst of that craziness I was discovering a gift—the gift of my own changed perspective. Because I had spent fifteen years living with this son of God's making, I saw so much more in Nathan than a hormone-crazed adolescent with issues. I saw that he had a generous heart. That he yearned to be a hero in his lifetime. That he longed to find meaning and purpose for his own crazy and different life. And that he tried hard in his own way to obey us and to grow into a responsible man. Step by halting step, Nathan was growing up.

And I was too!

I was learning life lessons that stretched my patience, increased my ability to love, showed me how very patient God was with my own imperfections, and gave me a resilience I would not have had. Besides, I loved loving my boy (at least most of the time). Even with his issues, he could be charming, charismatic, hilarious, and intriguing. Life was never dull with Nathan. He put the bubbles in the champagne of our life.

God had been teaching me these lessons ever since He first entrusted me with this amazing though different child. Minute by minute, year by year, I had learned to see with the eyes of my heart, to take my time before reacting or giving trite admonitions to this passionate soul. I had learned to walk this path of motherhood by faith, to guess how I needed to respond to Nathan in a healthy way.

My quiet times—times spent in prayer and studying God's Word—were lifelines through these years. Again and again I sought God's input about issues that tried my patience and made me feel like a failure. Again and again I asked forgiveness for my failures with Nathan—even my occasional inability to give him mother love. I even begged for the physical strength and energy I needed to parent this high-octane child. And God responded. Slowly He taught me to walk this journey of mothering this different child by faith that our heavenly Father had him in His hands. And slowly I learned to tune in to the voice of One who whispered words of challenge and blessing.

What if raising Nathan is an act of service I have called you to? Will you accept him as a gift from Me? Will you submit to the circumstances he brings to your whole family because you believe I am in control? Will you humble yourself and accept My will and cease to fight against him? Even if no one else ever sees the battles you have lived through or knows your quiet faithfulness to love him and to believe forward into his life? Your service of worship to Me is not lost. I see you! You may feel alone because so few understand, but you are not alone. I am with you and with him every day.

Nathan is fearfully and wonderfully made. He is different because I allowed it. He has My fingerprints all over his heart, mind, and soul—and his personality is a gift, not only a challenge.

By the time Nathan reached his turbulent teen years, those years of listening and learning helped us know how to respond to him—at least most days. Sympathetic love and acceptance of his quirks proved foundational to opening and reaching Nathan's heart. But discipline and training for righteousness were also foundational. Our son might have been different, but he still needed both limits and instruction. In fact, he might have needed these more than other children. So Clay and I worked hard to find a balance between open-hearted acceptance of Nathan's differences and holding firm on important issues, training him in character and values one day at a time.

Once Nathan questioned our decision not to let him go to a certain party. It was to be held at the home of a young man we knew was a troubled youth, with the possibility of drugs involved. The part of the argument I remember clearly took place in my little library behind closed doors, with us both standing to our full height, glaring, Nathan now towering above me at six foot three.

"The Clarksons are the *most idealistic family that has ever lived!*" he yelled at the top of his lungs.

"And you are a Clarkson!" I yelled back. "So you have to live within our ideals too!"

Those teenage years held lots of frustration, more than one slammed door, and hours and hours of talking, often until after midnight. Battles involving emotional health, spiritual ideals, and moral choices were hard fought, hard won, occasionally lost. Yet with time invested, a compassionate heart to hear Nathan's voice, intentional validation of his ideas and feelings, plus about a thousand chocolate chip cookies to sweeten conversation and frequent back rubs to soften attitudes, Clay and I earned the ability to challenge Nathan without losing him. Our engagement in who he was kept him coming back to foundations that had been laid. We were not always aware of this at the time, however. It was all by faith that we would not lose him in the face of peer pressure and his longing to fit in.

Nathan's particular form of difference meant he struggled all the time with germs, meals, machines, guilt, clothes, school, colors of things (yes, this was a big thing with him), authority, arguing, laziness, and excuses—to name a few.

With his big and occasionally explosive personality, he was often too much for people he met.

Because of my own challenges in being understood, I knew this was a burden he bore every day of his life. Finding fault with everything Nathan did would surely overwhelm him, as it would have done with me. Gradually it dawned on me that God did not show me all of my selfish issues and shortcomings at one moment. Instead, He graciously allowed me to mature over a lifetime—little by little, one shortcoming at a time.

So I learned to pick our battles carefully. I tried to focus on those things that mattered spiritually, not minor issues or man-made rules. I intentionally pressed in on issues that would affect relationships, character, and faith and tried to back off of other, less crucial issues (such as those baggy pants, worn without a belt, that drove me crazy on a daily basis).

Eventually I developed a little acronym, LAUNCH, to help me keep all this straight in my mind. It was not a magical formula that had to be followed, but it helped me to arm myself daily with what I would need to be an adequate mom to Nathan. It empowered me to shape my reactions to his constantly changing needs and eruptions. It helped me hold a vision for my goal as his parent—not to "fix" him or make him "normal," but to launch him into life as a healthy, self-actualized young man whose faith was intact and who had a solid emotional and moral grounding. I would do this by:

- Loving him with the love of God
- Affirming him daily, believing in who he will become
- Understanding his limitations and learning to be patient with his disability
- Never passing on guilt to him for being limited
- Changing his heart gradually through training in character and inner strength
- Holding expectations loosely and leaving him in the hands of God

Each time I whispered this "launch code" to myself, I reminded myself what my purpose in mothering Nathan was. Even in those moments—and there were many—when I was convinced God had chosen the least qualified person possible to be Nathan's mother, I still would plant a flag and make my stand: "I will mother Nathan for the glory of God. I will seek to win his heart for Christ and show him the unconditional love of God so that he will find it easier to believe in Him."

Such moments of decision—choosing one more time to follow my commitment—were required of me over and over. And each one of those moments prepared me for the moment when Nathan called me downstairs for his "big surprise."

By the time Nathan painted his room, I had developed a kind of grid in my mind for responding to him. I deliberately looked for ways to affirm him, to listen to his heart cry for me to believe in his dreams. I was predisposed to look into the hallways of his heart in order to love him as God loves him.

Even so, as I walked down the stairs, I had no idea what to expect. Knowing Nathan, it could be anything. So I took a deep breath and intentionally drew on what I had learned over the years. I remember telling myself, *Decide to see the surprise from his eyes. Decide to love him and affirm him . . .*

When I walked into his room, I was stunned. Nathan had not just decorated his new room. He had completely covered the pristine white walls and ceiling with multicolored swirls. Though I had not expected this, I was not totally surprised. Nathan often brought adventuresome moments to my life, and he did it with total enthusiasm.

He looked at me expectantly. And at that moment God seemed to whisper, *This is important to Nathan. He is revealing something profoundly important to him—an unusual, fervent, and generous expression of who he really is. You are privileged to enter into his soul revelation and to affirm the amazing man that he is becoming. He chose you to entrust with his dreams, his inner self. This is a sacred moment. Handle it with care and graciousness. Look deeply and listen to what his room is speaking to you.*

I remember staring at the mural as well as a watercolor he had made of Superman catching a bullet and seeing with my heart, perhaps for the first time, that this mysterious son of mine was a deeply creative artist. He was a dreamer, a storyteller, an inspirer. His work taught me to see him even more clearly. And this revelation of his artistic nature granted me a window into his world. It revealed aspects of his life I had not truly seen before.

But the last surprise I glimpsed spoke more powerfully to me than all the artwork he had created. Written in large blue letters on a piece of blue-bordered poster board, next to a five-foot Knights Templar warrior sword we had gifted him when he turned thirteen, were the words, "I will be God's." I saw this as a sincere expression from deep inside Nathan, a heart statement of his desire to follow hard after God his whole life and fight darkness with light and courage, a "come to Jesus" moment that I believe defined the commitment he wanted to make for life.

When I looked at that poster (which still hangs in his room today), all the irritations, the failures, the confrontations melted in insignificance. All the challenges of being different and parenting our very different boy faded away. Though I knew we would face unimagined challenges ahead and deal with new heartbreak as well as blessing, nothing else seemed as important as those four words.

Always I had hoped and longed for Nathan to understand that he had a role to play in his world, in God's megastory of life—that he would play a part no one else could play.

Now I knew that he did understand. And he embraced it with all the outsized passion that made him uniquely and beautifully Nathan.

And as long as my sweet, different, outside-the-box boy understood that indeed *he was God's*, I knew that everything would be all right.

CHAPTER 4

Harnessing a Hero

....

Character Training through Stories and Inspiration

NATHAN

I was never very good at focusing on anything for much longer than five minutes. That made solo reading an almost impossible task. Knowing this, my parents thought it would be a good idea to get audiobooks for me. These enabled me to sit and listen while I drew pictures or fiddled with other toys. Over the years a plethora of stories entered my heart through the inviting narrators' voices. But one story in particular stood out—Walter Farley's *The Black Stallion*.

It's the story of an untrained horse who befriends a teenager named Alec. "The Black" is stronger, faster, and smarter than all the other horses. But because of his unruly nature and unbridled personality, he is unable to compete in the races.

Alec can see the stallion's potential. He knows that if all the Black's raw power could be harnessed and focused through training, the horse could be a champion. So we follow the journey of Alec and the Black as the young man with love and firmness trains the stallion, as the horse allows his will to be harnessed, and as the two join together to win an important race.

I enjoyed the story very much as a boy, but it wasn't until I narrated the story back to my mom that I truly connected with it.

"You're a lot like that stallion," she said to me one summer day.

"I am?" I asked.

"Nathan, you have natural power, strength, skill, and a wild spirit that makes you hard to hold down—which is a good thing, but sometimes gets you into trouble . . ."

I stood in silence, thinking.

"The black stallion had to learn to accept reins and the commands of his master in order to access his amazing speed to win the race. And Nathan, if you allow yourself to be trained, if you accept the 'reins' of discipline and teaching, you can be a champion too!" My mom ruffled my hair and smiled her impish mama smile as if to say, "I know what I am talking about."

I let the words sink in, furrowing my young brow as I accepted the truth of the parallel.

....

I walked slowly to our book-filled den, soaking up every last second of freedom I could before the lessons I dreaded. I gazed out the window to our backyard, which stretched for miles toward the Texas hills. I longed to be out there under the burning Texas sun and the giant billowing clouds—roaming the fields, building forts, and fighting imaginary foes.

But alas, my short walk had brought me into the room with Mom and my siblings. Next to Mom was a pile of books big enough to make any six-year-old like me tremble in his sweatpants.

"Take a seat, Nathan, and let's get started."

I plopped down on a small sofa and tried to ready myself for the doom of one more anxious hour.

My mom picked up what looked to be about a million-page book. It was called *The Children's Homer: The Adventures of Odysseus and the Tale of Troy.*[3]

"Can you be quiet and listen? You can move around a little if it helps you—as long as you listen."

I nodded so as to get started sooner. She opened the book and began.

For the first few minutes I was doing well. Some of the characters were interesting, and I was following along.

But then, as the seconds turned to minutes, a song I had heard on the radio popped into my mind without any warning. I looked down and saw my foot tapping in the air like it had a mind of its own. It moved and swayed almost uncontrollably. Then I felt the movement work its way up my leg and slowly throughout the rest of my body. I couldn't be still.

I pushed my hands down deep in the couch cushions and twisted my body until I was upside down, head hanging off the sofa. I looked at the ceiling and began imagining what it would be like to walk upside down with no gravity. Suddenly my mind changed channels—a very familiar experience—and I began thinking about what my best friend, Jason, and I were going to do when we hung out next. Then, again changing channels, my mind started going through the best ways to build a fort outside. I felt my hand start tapping my chest, making a funny sound, and then suddenly—

"Nathan!" This sounded like maybe it was not the first time my name had been called. My mind came crashing back to earth. I was still upside down, so I had to look up to see my mother's concerned face.

"Do you remember what I asked you?" she said.

"To try to be quiet and listen." I realized I had failed once more at the only task given to me.

"Can you please try to be just a little quieter and be less distracting to the others?"

I slowly pulled myself around and back into a seated position, ready for round two to begin.

I tried my hardest. I really did. But my body and mind didn't seem to want to cooperate, and by round five I could tell my mother was losing her patience.

Later that night, as Mom was tucking me into bed, I told

her I wanted to listen and hear the stories, but my mind just wouldn't let me.

She gave me a concerned smile, fully aware of her little boy's shortcomings, no doubt, and unsure where the line was between understanding and discipline. Then she gently stroked the hair from my eyes and said, "The heroes in these books I want to read to you have things to overcome, just like you. But they are valiant warriors who face their enemies. They are brave like you are. We'll find a way for you to get to know them."

The next morning I walked to the den for another try. Everything in me wanted to be "good" and sit still and listen, but no matter how hard I tried, it seemed my mind and body refused to be subdued. So my stomach clenched with dread as I rounded the corner and saw my mom with book in hand. But this time there was more: a package of twenty-four sharpened colored pencils.

"What are those for?" I asked, surprised.

"I know that sitting still is hard for you, so I thought that today you might like to draw while I read."

I nodded apprehensively.

"But," she added, "I want you to draw the characters from the story while I read. Can you do that?"

Again I nodded, feeling a little better. I sat down and opened my drawing pad. I smoothed my fingers across a blank sheet that waited to hold epic scenes I had yet to imagine. Then I picked up a pencil.

My mom began reading. I let the pencil fly across the

paper. And miraculously, now that I had a task to focus on, I found I was somehow able to sit still. My mind didn't change channels, either. So as the stories my mother read about the hero Odysseus came to life on the pages in front of me, they also began going deep in my heart.

And that was the beginning of my fascination with stories—stories of truth and bravery, stories of heroes who, like me, had their own battles to fight, even though mine was simply a battle of sitting still. Day by day, read-aloud session by read-aloud session, I allowed myself to fall deeper and deeper into the narratives. The hero story arcs were so ingrained in my head, they worked their way into my soul. I began to see myself as a hero too, embarking on my own tale of courage and possibilities.

But this was only possible because of my mother's creativity and persistence. Fully aware of my limitations, she invited me into the stories in a way she knew I could respond to. Sometimes there were piles of Legos to play with, a box full of army figurines to act out the story, a snack to munch, a puzzle to put together. But from that time on, I always had something to occupy my hands, and that helped my mind to engage.

Mom could have tried to force me to sit still, creating more tension between us—and teaching me very little.

She could also have gotten mad and given up altogether, depriving us of a closer relationship and me of the stories I needed to inspire and encourage me.

But she knew how important the stories were going to

THE STORIES OF HEROES WERE SO
INGRAINED IN MY HEAD THAT THEY WORKED
THEIR WAY INTO MY SOUL.

be to me, so when she faced the challenge of a six-year-old boy with ADHD, she didn't force me to conform to a mold I was never meant to fit. She didn't get mad or simply give up. Instead, she met me where I was. And with a simple pad of paper and a collection of pencils, she made it possible for me to do what I needed to do.

She trained me, just as Alec trained the black stallion. And like the Black, I got better. Gradually I learned to sit a little longer, to accept the reins of my mom's making. And from then on I raced to story time, eager to engage with yet another heroic tale, and building patterns in my heart to remember even as I grew into a man.

Sally

When I was a girl, I loved to curl up in my four-poster double bed, pull the covers high on a cold winter night, and dream awake for hours. My dreams were fueled by the books I was reading and the epic films I loved to view—biographies of kings and queens, stories of heroes in battle, novels featuring strong, courageous heroines. Those stories inspired me to yearn for a future that involved more than just getting a job or finding a romantic partner in life. I wanted to do something important, to leave my mark on history. I wanted my life to count.

This desire for purpose, this deep longing to live a meaningful life, no doubt determined my later choices—even accepting a mission to a Communist country when I was twenty-three.

I believe that the longing to live a meaningful life resides inside all people. Not everyone is motivated by epic tales, by swords and swashbuckling and high romance. But each of us has the deep desire to become a hero in our own story—the person we were meant to be, accomplishing what we were created to accomplish. And I am convinced that each of us is designed to play a significant role in the history of the world. God created us with the personality, strengths, weaknesses, passions, and preferences we need to play our part. But to do that, most of us need inspiration. And stories can give us that.

There's a reason the Bible is full of stories. It's because God knows how powerful they can be. Stories are effective motivators. They can capture the imagination and awaken possibilities. They can give us something to aspire to and warn us of what to avoid.

Stories, in other words, have the power to shape our lives. And stories turned out to be the key to reaching our outside-the-box little boy.

As Nathan grew, I came to realize that he had a hero heart just like I'd had. And one day it dawned on me that if I could harness Nathan's love for hero tales and inspire him with tales of courage and bravery, I might be able to help him advance both personally and academically.

As long as I can remember, Nathan has been acting out stories that capture his imagination. He would brandish his toy sword and wield it high when he played outside on our old wooden swing set. He would act out a cavalry charge with a run through the yard and even enlist other kids to join him.

These activities kept Nathan engaged for many hours and were a godsend for both of us. Not only did they give him an outlet for his boundless energy and a way to exercise his mind and imagination, but they also gave me a much-needed break from his demands and the opportunity to get some of my other work completed.

I had always avoided allowing Nathan (and my other children) the crutch of too much "screen time"—TV, video games, computers, and so on. But that meant I needed to be resourceful about offering creative and engaging alternatives to fill their time. So I did my best to fill our home with what I call "tools of imagination"—games, supplies, and materials that would engage their interest and help them grow in thinking skills and imagination as they played.

This is where our dress-up box came in. We took a large chest we had found at a garage sale and filled it with props for imaginative play. (We could just throw everything in it and close the lid if we needed the place to be neatened up for visitors.) Dress-up clothes for the trunk often came from secondhand stores and garage sales—camouflage army pants, boots, dresses, costume jewelry, hats, and accessories. I created simple capes out of fabric remnants that could also serve as skirts, shawls, or other garments—providing hours of pretending to be superheroes and knights, princesses and waifs. And we collected lots of "gear"—plastic swords and shields, helmets and binoculars, baskets, play money, even a pipe so someone could pretend to be a detective like Sherlock Holmes.

That trunk was a wonderful resource for story-loving Nathan. I would occasionally give him five to ten dollars (usually as a reward for reading) and take him to a second-hand shop so he could shop for his own special props. Sometimes I would even back my car out of the garage to provide him a space where he could build tents and play areas and construct his own workshop for plays.

Imaginative play became so important to Nathan that when we moved, we looked for homes that would more easily accommodate it. We wanted yards where he could explore and play, giving me some extra time and tiring him enough to be able to sit still and listen or read.

As my extroverted son, Nathan always preferred playing with others, and he proved to be good at recruiting others for his activities. He could organize other boys to follow him like a pied piper, especially if it involved physical activity outside. I remember once looking out the window to see Nathan leading about twelve kids from the neighborhood through a homemade obstacle course.

Thinking of ways to occupy Nathan during quiet or alone times—neither of which were his preference—was a little more challenging. As the years progressed and he was able to sit still longer, he enjoyed listening to audiobooks ("books on tape," as we called them then). And we contin-ued to read together. Every day I would have all the kids go to their rooms or to a designated room in the house to read. I provided each of them with a basket full of interesting books in every genre: picture books, art and science books, classical literature, biographies, fiction. When they finished these books, I would treat them to some fun outing as a reward—to get frozen yogurt, to shop at the dollar store, or to play at the park with friends.

Because Nathan had such trouble reading, he and I usually read out loud together. (He especially responded to tales of people—historical or fictional—who achieved great accomplishments against great odds—people who fought off darkness and brought light.) Then he would sometimes use our tape recorder to create radio dramas based on the stories we had explored together.

There were plenty of days, of course, when Nathan (or my other kids) just could not sit at all without complaining, being noisy and argumentative, or generally creating havoc. But reading aloud was the most captivating subject he could manage, so that was the first thing we did after breakfast and devotions. I wanted to get Nathan on this important subject while he was the least tired.

As important as academic training was for Nathan, character training was even more important. I saw Nathan as a boy with great capacity for mental muscle, emotional muscle, spiritual muscle, and relational strength, but we needed to help him see this potential too and instill the confidence he needed to keep working toward that potential.

"Mom and Dad cannot make you strong inside," we told him. "We believe there is a hero inside of you waiting to come out. But you have to decide to be strong and then practice using *all* your muscles, inside and out, to grow into one."

Giving Nathan small steps for becoming strong inside helped him grow in this area. Setting clear boundaries and then working with him slowly, consistently, every day to follow those directives helped him to develop strength of character, a solid work ethic, and a dependable moral compass. This took years and years of moving one day at a time in the direction of self-control, maturity, kindness in relationships, and joy in his love of God.

Even as the trainer in the *Black Stallion* story saw potential in this powerful horse, so I saw endless potential in my wild, outside-the box little boy. My challenge was to balance accepting him just as he was while guiding him to grow. If I wanted him to be all he could be—all God created him to be—I needed to see both his realities and his possibilities and then keep my eyes on what God could accomplish. Then I needed to invest my energies into training my little boy, expanding his horizons one day at a time, one small step at a time.

Despite the inevitable stresses of raising a child like Nathan, I believe that God, Clay, and I turned out to be a formidable team. God had chosen us to be Nathan's parents. And God would be faithful to do more in all of our children's lives because He was with us. That was His promise.

What shall we say about such wonderful things as these? If God is for us, who can ever be against us?

ROMANS 8:31, NLT

I can do everything through Christ, who gives
me strength.

PHILIPPIANS 4:13, NLT

Train up a child in the way he should go,
Even when he is old he will not depart from it.

PROVERBS 22:6

One of our most useful tools for training Nathan and
our other children was a curriculum Clay created called *Our
24 Family Ways.*[4] Its purpose was to help our children learn
just what our standards and rules were for home life. These
24 Ways were posted prominently at home, discussed daily at
the breakfast table, and referenced even more often. All of our
children learned that because we were Clarksons, we treated
others with kindness, gentleness, and respect; we honored
our parents; we worked diligently at what we were given to
do; and so on. And when any of us failed to live up to our
24 Ways—as we all did frequently—we asked forgiveness,
corrected our mistakes if we could, and moved forward. The
emphasis was never on perfection, but on helping each other
become who we were meant to be within a family setting.

Up until the last hundred years or so, most education and
training was home based, at least in the early years. Children
worked side by side with their parents to learn not only skills,
but character. Often children would grow up to adopt the
family profession as well—farmers' children became farmers, blacksmiths' children became blacksmiths, and so on.

Little ones grew into their potential because of home life, not because of an arbitrary standard of education.

We wanted that for our children—Nathan included. Personally, I loved the idea of mentoring them. It became my delight to capture their imagination by reading them the greatest stories of literature, to take them with us when we traveled so they could meet people from every walk of life and many nationalities, to teach them to serve others and cultivate friendships by hosting people in our home, and to provide tools with which they could build their own creative muscle.

Especially important to me was to pass on a picture of the living God—showing His deep love, celebrating His divine artistry in creation, helping my children understand the purposes for which each of us was made, providing an emotional foundation for what I would teach. I especially wanted my different children to hear words from me and from Scripture that would deeply shape the pathways of their minds, instilling a confidence that God was on their side, that God had a place for them in writing the history of the world, that they were suited to live into a great story.

So our personal family story was written through days of teaching, training, and celebrating life that required not only patience and diligence, but also thoughtfulness, creativity, and a willingness to engage in cultivating a home alive with imagination, a delightful environment for learning and developing a love of learning.

And all was based on a foundation of prayer: *God, we believe You live in our home. Do a miracle with our small work of parenting our children as best we can and prepare them to be Yours for Your Kingdom work. We know that You will do exceedingly above all that we ask or think. Please be the life, the light, the wisdom, the love that fills our home and the strength for us to be faithful.*

A childhood of hearing and acting out stories has now turned Nathan into a story man. He writes scripts that touch hearts, produces films that matter, writes books to inspire his generation. And all that began at home, with our attempts to give him something great to believe in and aspire to. We sowed the best we could and depended on God to step in where we failed. And as a result, Nathan is harvesting a life built on faith and inspiration.

[Jesus] said to me, "My grace is sufficient for you, for my power is made perfect in weakness." Therefore I will boast all the more gladly about my weaknesses, so that Christ's power may rest on me.

2 CORINTHIANS 12:9, NIV

CHAPTER 5

A Heart like Superman

Living into a Higher Purpose

NATHAN

I walked out of the theater and into the warm April evening. Night had fallen over Los Angeles in the almost three hours I had been inside watching the most recent summer block-buster. But something else was different—I felt it.

Most of my recent nights had been spent sequestered away inside my one-room apartment, trying to just get through another day in what was proving to be the hardest of my twenty-six years. Recently I had had a falling out with my best friend and ended up leaving my church. I was essentially alone in the overwhelming city of Los Angeles. And then in recent months, severe anxiety had brought my ever-present OCD to an all-time high.

So it was something of a miracle I had even made it out of my apartment to begin with. I had no close friends I felt strong enough to see, and the angst of being out in an uncontrollable world often seemed unbearable in those days. But something in me told me I had to break out of the walls I had been hiding behind, even if it was just for a few hours by myself to see a superhero flick.

But this wasn't a random choice. Since I was a young boy, superheroes had always held a special place in my heart. And even now, something about them drew a childlike excitement in me.

As I made my way back to the parking garage with the images of those Marvel characters still flashing through my mind, I began, as I had done so many years ago, imagining myself as the star of my own superhero story, fighting bad guys and saving the day. The closest things to bad guys I was fighting at that time were an unruly mind and a broken heart. But I still found myself caught up in the what-ifs of living a story like the one I had been watching.

Something grabbed my attention as I passed the closed American Eagle Outfitters store. I stopped and stared into the dark retail store display at the tall man staring back at me. It actually took me a minute to realize I was seeing my own reflection, because the man in the window looked very different from the man who had gone into that theater. My shoulders were no longer slumped. My back was straight, my chest puffed out—I stood at my full height.

This was a side of myself I hadn't seen in a long time.

Life had been warring on me, and my out-of-control thoughts had served to pull my head down. But as I looked at this man reflected in the window, I caught a glimpse of the Nathan who had heroes on his mind. A man with head held high, ready to take on the world and save the day.

Maybe I can't fly through the air, I thought as I drove home that night. *But maybe I can make it through one more day.*

....

The excitement was rising in my thirteen-year-old heart as the miles passed beneath me and my family as we made our way into Illinois. Behind us was home and hundreds of miles of listening to audiobooks, singing five-part harmony to Rich Mullins CDs, sharing M&Ms, and gazing out at the seemingly endless fields of middle America. But ahead was the highly anticipated and what I believed to be magical town of Metropolis, home of Superman.

Yes, I knew it was just a little town in southern Illinois. But it was a town that had embraced my favorite childhood hero as enthusiastically as I had. They had a Superman museum there and a three-story statue of the Man of Steel. So in my mind Metropolis had become a place of pilgrimage. I couldn't wait.

We rounded one last corner, and the Superman statue came into view—an unmissable presence in front of the town hall. The car slowed to a stop, and I eagerly threw the door open and jumped outside. For an extended pause I just stood there taking in the larger-than-life red, blue, and yellow figure.

NATHANMAN!

I thought back to the time leading up to this moment. During the months previous, I had found myself daily hurrying through my schoolwork, counting the minutes to the afternoon of escape into a hero world. I could race to my bedroom and eagerly push Play on the portable DVD player on my bed to watch my favorite superhero in action. As the bright colors and heroic acts passed across the screen, they raced beyond just my eyes and into my heart.

To most, Superman is simply another piece of pop culture—entertaining, mildly amusing, perhaps even a little hokey. But not to me. Superman is my longtime hero, so much more than just a fictional character. From the time I first heard about Superman, his was a symbol I longed to inhabit, a story I wanted to embrace for myself.

Like young Clark Kent, I realized at an early age that I didn't act the way most others did, I couldn't do all the things that others could do, and I saw the world very differently than those around me did. Long before I had names for my differences, they shaped me and often left me feeling very alone.

I would look at my siblings and the people around me and wonder why ordinary school subjects such as math and reading came so hard to me. Why others seemed to effortlessly understand things I simply could not.

I wondered why I found it so hard to stop moving when everyone else could sit still. Why was I always getting in trouble when others were able to just "be good"? Was I bad? Was I messed up? Did God make a mistake when He created me? I would wonder these things as I lay in bed at night, wishing I could just be normal.

But on those afternoons when I escaped to my room to lose myself in the Superman stories, I began finding comforting similarities between me and the Man of Steel. As I watched Clark Kent struggle with being different while learning how to use his secret powers for good, I wondered if perhaps all the things that made me different could be used for good in the story I was going to tell with my life. Maybe these tics and "disabilities" were actually a sort of power given to me by God to be used to save the world.

Maybe the unbridled energy I felt that made it hard to sit still would be used to keep on going when others stopped.

Maybe my need to always talk back and question things, which constantly got me in trouble, could be honed into new forms of creativity.

And maybe my overwhelming anxiety helped me think more deeply about how life is meant to be lived.

I didn't know, but I certainly hoped so.

And as I sat curled up in bed with my portable DVD player, eyes wide, watching Superman save the day—not in spite of his differences but because of them—I would suddenly find hope that I could live the life of a hero.

....

Good stories are powerful. They serve to invigorate, teach, and inspire those who take part. Jesus changed the entire world with the stories He told as He walked around His homeland.

But *why* are stories so effective? What is it about exposing ourselves to tales of courage or high wisdom or great beauty that has the power to change us?

I can't really answer for other people, but I know what stories do for me.

Stories put me in the context of something bigger than myself and help me see my day-to-day struggles as enemies to overcome for the sake of a greater purpose. Whether as a teenager dealing with mental illness or a young adult struggling with the anxiety of living alone in a big city, I have found these tales help remind me that I myself am living a story. That every little experience or decision I make affects the meaning and the outcome. Which means I have a choice in what kind of story my life will tell.

Will I choose to be a victim of my circumstances, using my differences and difficulties as excuses for why I failed to do great things? Or will I decide to view my differences as superpowers that can enable me to live better and live out a story worth telling?

Sally

One evening when Nathan was three and a half, we told the boys to put on their very best armor because we were going to act out a Bible story together. Nathan had no trouble obeying this request. He loved performing and pretending.

"Do you think you would be brave enough to fight against a giant almost three times your size?" Clay asked when they were finished digging through the dress-up box. "Goliath was a huge giant who yelled and threatened thousands of soldiers in the Jewish army."

Uncharacteristically, Nathan was rapt with attention.

"But there was a young boy named David who was much smaller than the giant, who thought he was courageous enough to face the giant enemy who threatened them. You see, when David was out in the wild desert lands of Israel, he protected his little sheep from a bear. Then he killed a lion that was trying to bother his sheep. David was a boy who believed that with God's help, he could do anything! Even conquer a giant!

"I think, with God by your side, you boys can conquer the giants that come into your lives."

Clay then read the story to our little crew. Nathan still sat focused, hearing this courageous tale for the first time with an innocent child's heart. At the end of the reading, Clay said, "Let's act this story out. I will be the giant, and Nathan, you can be David first!"

And so my very introverted husband mounted up with a plastic sword and shield held high and boomed at Nathan, who stood as tall as his three-year-old self could muster.

Clay stomped his feet as he walked toward Nathan.

"You are so small. You have no strength. What makes you think you can fight me? *Are you a coward?*"

Nathan, brandishing his sword high, summoned his

courage. He scowled fiercely and yelled out as loudly as he could muster: *"Yes, I am!"*

He did not know what a coward was, but he was going to be it with all his heart.

The rest of the family fell to the ground, giggling, while Nathan looked around in confusion. He had no idea what had happened. But we did tell him we thought he would be a great warrior, just like David.

Nathan just beamed when he heard that. He's always loved the idea of being a hero. He *needed* to be a hero because it took a special helping of courage and energy for him just to get through his life.

When he was just a bit older, he discovered superheroes, especially Superman. And from the time he learned about the Man of Steel, he wanted to *be* the Man of Steel. He made good use of the bright blue cape I had made him by "flying" around the yard and acting out the exploits of his favorite superhero.

"Mom," he would say wistfully, his eyes serious with intent, "Superman is like Jesus. He came from a far-off place, and he helped people who needed rescuing."

The more I thought about it, the more it made sense. The story of Superman is essentially the story of an outsider—an alien—who had the ability to make a big difference in the world, even though most people around him had no clue who he really was. I understood the heart of Nathan's comparison and realized he was beginning to understand what the coming of Jesus meant. And to be totally honest, I think both Jesus and Superman are excellent role models for a different boy or girl with the heart of a hero.

....

As I have mentioned, it took me a while to finally begin understanding the many issues that challenged Nathan daily in his little-boy world. I did not have the resources or friends or materials that are available now to understand his differences. I mostly had a lot of critics who made me feel like a failure as a mom. So I was left to try to figure out my Nathan all on my own, through lots of prayer and lots of trial and error.

Even as a toddler, he had troublesome issues. When he was about eighteen months old, I would put his little red tennis shoes on him every day and begin to tie them. And every day he would throw a fit—a real fit, with incomprehensible screaming and rolling around on the floor. I dreaded daily the moment I would have to put those shoes on. I had no idea what was creating such an extreme response from my little guy.

Then one day, by accident, I tied his shoestrings with a bow the same exact length on both sides. He sighed deeply and said, "Oh, tank you, Mama." And I realized—though I still didn't understand why—that if I tied the laces the exact same length, he could be calm and move ahead into his day.

Many years later, when Nathan's OCD was finally diagnosed, I would look back at that memory and finally understand that moment.

Nathan was different, in other words, from the very beginning, and we needed to accept that. But Nathan was also God's handiwork, with the imprint of God on his soul. So I began to pray that God would give us eyes to see his value, his skills, his heart so that we could figure out how to reach him and to help him succeed. And that was tricky, because Nathan's differences made it hard for him to accomplish what other children did with ease.

He clearly had a bright, inquisitive mind—no one could ask more questions than Nathan! He loved stories and pretending, ideas and arguing, and his arguments could sometimes be quite persuasive. He was also physically graceful and surprisingly charismatic, able to rally groups of other kids for his elaborate games. But his arguments easily devolved into contention and fights, his questions could be aggressive and confrontational, and the smallest (to us) challenge could trigger a monumental emotional meltdown.

Anything systematic or rules-oriented—spelling, grammar, classroom regulations—posed big problems for Nathan. And any form of math was almost a lost cause. No matter what we did, two plus two rarely equaled four. We persevered, however, and made some progress. Many years later, after writing a movie and producing it himself, Nathan had to organize his payroll to give to the accountant. It was a struggle, but he did a fine job.

In public settings or classes, of course, Nathan wiggled excessively and often got in trouble. Teachers would take us aside and say, "Nathan doesn't seem to be able to control himself in normal classroom situations. I think maybe he needs you to discipline him more . . ." Negotiating these kinds of situations became a way of life for me as Nathan's mom. Sometimes shame or discouragement swept over me—especially since I had no clue how to change the situation. Feelings of inadequacy would follow me through the years.

....

In Nathan's elementary-age years, we began to suspect that he might suffer from attention deficit/hyperactivity disorder—ADHD. Nathan was always on the go, never sat still, had difficulty concentrating, and was somewhat overpowering in his interaction with adults. These characteristics fit many of the symptoms of ADHD described in material I was reading about children with differences. I asked friends, teachers, and doctors to observe Nathan, and many agreed that this was one of his issues. When he was in his teens, we would consult learning specialists who confirmed this diagnosis.

I had heard that little boys like him were often given medication such as Ritalin to calm them down. But as I prayed about this solution and researched it, I had misgivings. I wanted to ponder and search out the scope of Nathan's unique issues before trying medication.

It seemed to me that in the area where we lived, a great number of children were being labeled prematurely and medicated just to make them easier to handle. And while I could sympathize with that desire, I wasn't sure it was always appropriate. Some children have developmental issues that will resolve themselves with greater maturity. Some just need more time to mature, fewer hours on machines, and some extra love and training.

Eventually we decided not to medicate Nathan for ADHD while he was young. We would wait and see how he developed. Please understand that I am not holding up this decision as a model for every parent to follow. I am not saying it's wrong to medicate for these kinds of issues. As Nathan grew older, proper medication would make a big positive difference in his life. I am just sharing how and why we made our decision with the limited information we had. I hope it's helpful. But you will have to choose for yourself after research, consultation, and careful observation, what is best for your own uniquely different child.

I will say that although Nathan had *many* ups and downs during those elementary years, I'm glad we waited until he was older to begin trying out medication. By working with him as he was, I was challenged to get creative and find ways to reach him. In the process I learned many techniques for helping him control himself and calm down enough to learn. Many of these he still finds helpful in his life today.

One of my other adult children told me recently that she thought a distinct aspect of my parenting style was that I sought to find unique places for my children to flourish based on each of their personalities and individual needs. Giving my kids freedom and grace to become their full selves was a precious value to me as a mom, and seeing the results in their adult lives has been highly gratifying. Somehow this looking for the heart instead of external performances set Nathan and my other children free to pursue their dreams.

....

As I prayed for Nathan and pondered him over the early years of his life, I gradually began to understand more fully that he was not a problem to be addressed, not the sum of his behavioral performance. His worth to God was not about his ability to fulfill other people's expectations or act according to accepted norms. Instead he was a beloved child of the Father with a specific role to play in God's ongoing story of redemption.

Again, this was a lesson long in coming. It hurt my feelings when people made no effort to understand what we were going through. I often felt humbled, discouraged, angry, lonely, and so very tired of dealing with these issues day in and day out, especially with three other children who needed me and other responsibilities mounting in my life. Daily I sought for wisdom, understanding, and insight into what would make our lives a bit easier and help all my children grow into their potential. And gradually I began to focus on two scriptural principles that helped me immensely.

Because of my many years in ministry, I had studied and written a lot about Jesus' relationship with His disciples. And I had noticed that one of the Master's relational strengths was His constantly speaking positive things into the lives of His followers:

- "Peter, you are the rock" (see Matthew 16:18).
- "Mary, you chose the good part" and (later)
  "Mary, your story will be told through generations
  because you have done this beautiful thing for Me"
  (see Luke 10:42 and Matthew 26:6-13).
- "Centurion, I have never seen greater faith in all
  of Israel" (see Matthew 8:10).
- "Nathanael, you are a man in whom there is
  no deceit" (see John 1:47).

That was one principle. The other emerged as I studied God's priority for His children throughout Scripture. I noticed a consistent theme: the importance of the heart.

- "People judge by outward appearance, but the LORD
  looks at the heart" (1 Samuel 16:7, NLT).
- "Love the Lord your God with all your heart"
  (Matthew 22:37).
- "The eyes of the LORD move to and fro throughout
  the earth that He may strongly support those whose
  heart is completely His" (2 Chronicles 16:9).

There are many, many verses like these throughout the Old and New Testaments. In fact, the heart is mentioned as a priority to God more than eight hundred times in Scripture. The overall implication is that God values the inner person—will, imagination, values, purpose, attitude—more than behavior or even beliefs.

That's not to say behavior and beliefs are unimportant. They are. But God seems to care most about who we are on the inside. He looks for a heart that is devoted to trusting Him and then strongly supports this person's life, work, and relationships, accomplishing far beyond what that person could do naturally.

Those two scriptural principles—speaking positive words into a life and focusing on heart issues—became my essential strategy for raising Nathan. We prayed regularly that God would help us figure out how to reach Nathan's heart with a vision for how God might use him. We wanted to build a world in Nathan's mind where he was not always the odd man out, the kid who could not perform to the expectations of others. He needed a sense of himself that was not based on math scores or behaving correctly inside four walls, but on integrity, moral character, and courageous action. He needed to find a way to be fully himself and yet be strong in ways that God would use.

That's when I began to collect "boy" books that had beautiful photos and great stories. That's when we began our special one-on-one reading times. And that's when Clay and I began a conscious practice of speaking words of affirmation and promise over our different boy.

- "Daniel was brave when he faced the lions because he believed God would protect him. Nathan, I think you are like Daniel."

- "Nathan, I think you can run around the yard faster than almost any boy your age I have seen. You are becoming so strong."
- "Nathan, I think God has given you a loving heart. You are so good to our sweet dog. Kelsey loves it when you throw her the ball. You are her special friend."
- "'Gift of God' is what your name means. With God's strength, you will go far, my Nathan. You are a hero in the making. I wonder how you will bring His light into this dark world, love people who need encouragement, inspire those who need hope. I can't wait to see how God uses your gifts to help others."

This kind of affirmation is important for all children, of course, but it's especially crucial for the Nathans of the world, who tend to push buttons and provoke negative feedback from others and who can easily lose heart as a result.

I admit that I've dished out plenty of that negativity myself—sometimes for the right reasons, and sometimes out of pure frustration. For instance, as a mom with loads of housework, meals to make, and details to attend to, not to mention my writing and ministry work, I expected our children to step up and help. And Nathan's capacity to do this proved much lower than the others'.

When the other children were given a small task, they could usually complete it without much fuss. With Nathan, however, tasks would rarely be completed quickly and often not at all. And that meant I was always correcting him. "You still haven't done your chores, and you always argue with your brother and sister—why can't you do it right the first time just once?"

Because Nathan did need to be trained, some of that correction was unavoidable. But when I put myself in Nathan's shoes, I realized that my constant correction could easily be a source of frustration, insecurity, and anger in my already-fragile child. That constant feeling of just not measuring up can build a lifelong legacy of insecurity and even despair. Feeling like a disappointment on a regular basis can actually shape the brain patterns of a growing child. Failure and helplessness can become self-fulfilling prophecies.

So how can the parents of a different child counter that tendency while still giving the child necessary guidance? Partly by choosing our battles, as I have already mentioned. (Not everything is worth a confrontation or even a correction.) But also by deliberately speaking forward, by faith, into the heart of the child.

I wanted to give Nathan a unique path on which he could succeed. I wanted him to have a sense of who he could be—not in comparison to siblings or to peers, but just as he was, by making the most of the positive qualities God had given him.

And so I made it a goal to try to say as many positive statements to him as I could—observations about his great personality, his huge capacity for love, his courage and potential. And I made a point of focusing on the inside qualities, the heart issues that could not be measured by a rule or behavioral performance. And with these observations I tried to include gentle nudges and direction to help him use those heart qualities.

The fable of the tortoise and the hare became a favorite story with a very specific application. "You are one of the most persistent people I know, and it is the one who is persistent that wins the race. If you practice being disciplined just a little bit every day, you will win the race of your life."

Then I would set the timer for fifteen minutes at a time. "Work and clean your room for fifteen minutes, and then you can go outside."

"Read for fifteen minutes and try to focus. When the timer goes off, you can tell me what you know. Then you can have a snack and listen to one of your stories on the tape recorder."

Consequently, even now, Nathan reads fifteen minutes a day and covers about six books each year little by little. He has ten-minute devotions and prayer times every day. Through these persistent habits, acquired as a young boy, he has acquired mental and spiritual strength.

From the time he was a little boy, I did my best to help Nathan live into his Superman dreams. I affirmed his desires and his character, provided him with understanding and gentle guidance, and saw him grow stronger just a tiny bit at a time.

I truly believed—and believe—that our *different* boy had the capacity to become a great man of God. And I told him so again and again, reminding him of what could happen if he based his faith in a great God, not on his ability or inability to perform for other people.

What a joy to see our observations and predictions come true in the life of a grown son I truly admire.

A man like David, who struggles.

But also like David, a man after God's own heart.

CHAPTER 6
The Grand Performance

....

The Therapy of Nature and Creation

NATHAN

The screen door glided open as I stepped out into a warm Colorado summer evening. A gentle wind rustled through my hair and ran beyond me from where I stood on our front deck into the pines and up the foothills into the mountains of the national forest near our house.

I turned my head to the east and saw the hills descend into the vast plains that stood as audience to the sun's fiery descent behind the Rockies.

In my eleven-year-old arms I held a jumble of blankets and pillows, which I threw confidently onto the floor of our front-porch deck. Behind me, inside, I heard the sounds of giggles and singing as my siblings and parents shuffled out beside me, followed by our curious golden retriever, Penny.

On this summer night we had decided to be adventurous. We were going to brave the wild outside our front door and sleep under the open sky. We all began claiming our spots on the deck and distributing blankets and pillows—my parents at the end of the row of excited kids.

For most in the world it was just another Friday night. But in our hearts we could feel the mysterious presence of something beautiful about to happen. As the sky slowly darkened from red to indigo, we excitedly talked amongst ourselves, reiterating our most interesting stories from the week. Penny wandered from pallet to pallet, licking faces and making sure we knew she was a part of the team.

As the hours wore on, talking faded to whispers and whispers into silence, until nothing could be heard but the sound of wind in the pines. Penny had settled down between me and Joy, my little sister. I realized I was the last one awake. Taking one more sweeping look at the darkened sky, I let my eyes fall shut and my body settle into a sweet sleep.

Suddenly my eyes popped open as a cool wind blew across my face. Drowsily I looked around to find my family was still asleep and Penny was still nestled at my side. The comfort of being close to those I loved best warmed me through, though the air around us was chilly. It must have been about three in the morning.

I LEARNED THAT THE SAME LOVING GOD
WHO ORCHESTRATED THE NIGHTTIME
SYMPHONY OF STARS CONTROLLED
THE DETAILS OF MY LIFE.

I put my head down and slowly turned to lie on my back. And suddenly I was confronted with a grand performance, as though the sky was dancing just for me. Above me was spread a magnificent array of stars, each shimmering in choreographed order.

When I was falling asleep earlier, I had seen them appearing one by one. But now they had gathered in their full force of infinite galaxies to light the sky. In dazzling formation they spread themselves across the black canvas of space, thousands upon thousands for my young eyes to behold. Intermittently a meteor would streak across the sky in a showy display.

I drew in my breath and tried to be completely still. And for a moment it seemed I could see the entire sky move.

I stared, awestruck, and let the silent but glorious moment sink in. How grand the universe was. How small I felt in comparison. How incredibly powerful and creative was the God I prayed to. And how amazing that He would conduct a grand performance just to fill my little-boy heart with wonder.

There are moments in life so beautiful that everything in us wants to praise the Creator. Maybe it's stars—or an ocean view, a magnificent sunset, the birth of a child. It's important to put ourselves in places and situations that bring us those moments—and to recognize them for what they are.

When I was growing up with my bundle of problems, I desperately needed times like the night I spent on my deck looking at the stars. To me they were a reminder that even though my struggles felt big and unbeatable, I followed a

God who was infinitely bigger and more powerful than any of them. I learned to let His infinite grandness assure my struggling heart that the same loving God who orchestrated the nighttime symphony of stars was in control of the details of my life.

What an amazing realization—that the One who cast the universe in motion cares about my struggle with washing my hands too many times.

That the One who made the stars is also the Father who created each of us unique, individually reflecting His creativity.

That the One who makes the sky move can also help our hearts be still.

May I never forget that lesson. May I always let that infinite grandness put my troubles in perspective as I walk through this world.

Sally

Four-year-old Joy, bedecked in a well-worn and slightly torn pink tutu, twirled round and round, her little feet echoing on our wooden deck with each swirl.

"Texas sheet cake, fried chicken, popcorn—yummies! And I get to have Penny sleep with me under the stars. Can't wait, can't wait, can't wait," she chanted.

The boys had been assigned to set up our sleeping places while Sarah made the cake and Joy just danced. I would have the futon mattress to provide a little bit of adult comfort while "roughing it" in our own front deck; Clay would sleep on a bed just inside the screen door, but just feet away. And everyone else would have to pile up blankets, sleeping bags, and pillows. Because of the cold mountain air, we would sleep practically on top of each other to keep warm.

"I wonder what God was thinking when He made cocoa beans? Surely He had Texas sheet cake in mind!" I commented as I pushed the screen door open with my foot and brought out the evening feast. "Did He know that corn would pop into fluffy balls when it was heated? And did He imagine that butter and salt would be the perfect toppings to make the popcorn absolutely delicious?" The answer was a cascade of giggles as everyone gathered round.

On nights like these, we took to heart the psalmist's invitation to "taste and see that the LORD is good" (Psalm 34:8). We would cuddle close, smack fried chicken, ooh and aah at a spectacular sunset, and rest away from the world of pressures and rules. The humming wind singing through the tops of the pine trees, the mountain jays squawking their own awkward songs, the aspens rattling a familiar rhythm would inspire the children to cartwheels and handstands. I would breathe deeply, enjoying their antics.

And then, when night fell, we would imagine out loud just what the stars and sky were singing about the God who made them:

The heavens proclaim the glory of God.
    The skies display his craftsmanship.
Day after day they continue to speak;

night after night they make him known.
They speak without a sound or word;
    their voice is never heard.
Yet their message has gone throughout the earth,
    and their words to all the world.

PSALM 19:1-4, NLT

Always and always we would point to a heavenly Father who was an artist, lover, servant, warrior, shepherd, and king. Always and always we looked for ways to help our children to understand they had been "fearfully and wonderfully made" by the artist God (Psalm 139:14).

....

Magical, mysterious, wonderful—those words describe the setting of our little Colorado home nestled against twenty-five thousand acres of national forest. Tucked away under the shadow of a massive stone giant of a mountain, we sat high on the hillside peeking down over the sparkling lights of the city below. The purple, pink, orange sunsets danced around our little home almost every night to add a blessing to the day's end.

Because our house was built on a mountain slope, our main floor was actually the second floor. The kitchen, living room, and master bedroom had been built high, with windows peering out on the forested land. A wooden deck ran the length of our home, so that we could access it from almost any door. And we loved that deck. At almost any hour of the day, it was our favorite place to be because it placed us outdoors against the strong, shadowy mountain and the swaying pines.

At seventy-five hundred feet above sea level, the deck was always cooled by crisp mountain air. The weathered picnic table, seating up to twelve people if we squished, was where we ate our meals every night of summer and fall. As the sun set, a hush would fall over the valley below, and the sparkle of thousands of lights in the city below added charm to our evening dinners.

That home proved to be an incalculable gift during the years when our children were moving toward adulthood. It was indeed a privilege to just step out of the house and breathe that pine-scented mountain air, to live where there was plenty of space for them to run free. During the two years we lived there, we always looked for opportunities to sleep outside or at least to sit out on a blanket under the stars at night. And memories of that special place have lasted us all a lifetime.

Not all our homes have been that idyllic, of course. Remember, we moved seventeen times when our kids were growing up, and we were rarely so fortunate as to have a mountain in our backyard! But we always tried to choose homes that were as close to nature as we could get, with the biggest yards we could afford. And even when we lived in small apartments overseas, we sought out parks and hiking trails on the edges of the city where we lived.

Giving our children a place to roam, run, play, and yell seemed essential. Nathan, especially, needed an outlet for his over-the-top energy, and being outdoors seemed a balm to his agitation and anxiety.

But there was also another reason we intentionally chose to place our family in a natural, rural setting. Nature displayed the fingerprints of God for each of us to remember His transcendence. He was far above our own finite lives, and to see His grandeur reminded us that as the heavens were higher than the earth, so were His ways higher than our ways and His thoughts higher than our thoughts (Isaiah 55:9, paraphrased from the NKJV).

We celebrated together the wonderful knowledge that in God's universe, we all had a place to belong, even if we sometimes had trouble fitting in at school, church, or social settings. Clay and I wanted our children to know without a doubt that the God who created our beautiful mountains had created them, too. Living free in the outdoors, running through mountains, and hiking on trails gave us relief from trying to fit into the boxes of the world's expectations.

Nathan, especially, loved the outdoors, and he loved being reminded that the God of creation had crafted him, too. His outsized personality, his clear blue eyes, his questioning mind, his booming voice, his bigger-than-life dreams—all were part of God's beautiful and unique design. And this same God listened to his cries, to his joys and his stories, and wanted to run through life with him every day.

....

I think my kids would all agree that our family adventures outdoors created some of our favorite family memories. Roaming the nearby hills and trails, making excursions to local parks or attractions, or simply playing in the yard together put us in closer touch with God and each other.

We also made a point of seeking out natural beauty when we traveled—the churning, endless oceans, grand and sweeping plains, breathtaking canyons and rock formations, lush forests, and vast, silent deserts under bright blue skies. Making the creativity of the living God part of the dance of our children's lives filled the memory boxes of their hearts with sweet pleasures. And our experiences helped us remember that His design for our planet was greater and bigger than we could imagine.

God was the first artist, after all, crafting masterpieces that would be discovered throughout all eternity. Exposing our children to His handiwork as often as possible was a priority for Clay and me. Placing our children (and ourselves) in the face of this creator God seemed to increase their sense of delight in Him and left a taste of pleasure in their souls. It also provided respite and relief from our stressful daily lives.

So much of our life as parents is focused on our children's external behavior: manners, speech, work ethic, accomplishments in school, respect. And all that training is vital for their future. But how wonderful it is to make time together when no outward performance is required—only play, love, fun, pleasure, and rest where we can all feel okay about making a mess—or being a mess. Our children need to live into the infinite possibilities of innovative ideas, symphonies of created music, breathtaking visual art, transcendent science, and thoughts of God that are too big to be contained by the walls of a church building.

For Nathan, those times when he could breathe out the fear of doing something wrong and breathe in the freedom and grace to be himself were a literal godsend. He desperately needed a regular time in a protected place without critics, and our family adventures gave him this. His little-boy wonder-soul always delighted in being out of doors, where he could whoop and holler to his heart's content. The other children felt that release as well. When our children ran and played outside, I always noticed there was less fussing.

Our nature excursions gave me a break as well, a chance to back off from managing a household and a business and just relax and play. I desperately needed times like that when I could breathe in peace and recover from my fraught days. In fact, finding ways to get outdoors was essential to my keeping a good, positive heart. When I got on my knees in the garden, discovered a new hiking trail in the woods, or simply watched my family play in the yard under a high-arched blue sky, I would remember that God was bigger than my issues, wiser than my limited knowledge, and both willing and able to carry my burdens.

I especially loved our at-home adventures on the deck. Convenient camping is what I called it. We did not even have to leave the house. I did not have to pack up the kitchen, gather camp clothes, or inconvenience myself in the least. I just had to slide some sleeping bags outside and make (or order!) one more meal.

Other outdoor adventures took more effort, of course—packing a picnic, preparing the car, planning itineraries. But getting out into nature and discovering different manifestations of God's creativity was always worth it. The work paid off enormously in terms of giving us all breathing room and a chance to replenish our spirits.

Whenever possible, we included our family dogs on our family adventures. Penny was just the latest in a parade of golden retrievers who shared our lives over the years. Having someone in our home who would love our children unreservedly, be excited to see them no matter what their behavior, and share their outdoor adventures became a priority and then a conviction through the years. (Even at this writing, we have recently acquired a new golden named Darcy Dog.)

I think those dogs might have been angels from God who spread love and affection generously every day, all the time, and they were absolutely a godsend to the mama of energetic boys. Joel and Nathan would curl up with them, throw balls to them endlessly, and expend lots of excess energy playing with them. (To this day, my boys love to wrestle with, play with, and snuggle with our newest retriever—the best free therapy a mama could hope for.)

....

Not everyone has the privilege of living in the mountains next to a national park, of course. (We don't live in that house anymore, either, although we do enjoy living in Colorado once again.) But all of us need to find ways to taste the Lord's goodness and spend time soaking in the beauty and variety of His creation. And such places are all around us, sometimes hiding in plain sight. Whether we live in tiny apartments or suburban subdivisions or out in the country, we can—and must—seek out places of refuge where we can all breathe fresh air and freedom. Walks in public parks, trips to national parks, fishing in a river, picnics in forests for a day away from the demands of daily life—any of these can restore souls. And we always have the option, with a little bit of ingenuity and maybe some packets of seeds, to create little havens of natural beauty right where we are. Even a basket of herbs on a high-rise balcony can lift our spirits. What matters is that we seek it out, that we make space for awe and wonder, rest and relaxation, beauty and creation in the middle of our busy lives.

We all need that.

Children need that—especially the different ones.

And busy, distracted mamas may need that most of all.

In the midst of our busy, stressful, challenging days, we desperately need to taste the beauty of the Lord and remember just how good He is.

I, too, tasted His goodness as we snuggled together on that deck in Colorado, under the myriad of sparkling, shooting stars. Even as I acknowledged my tininess in comparison to the galaxies above, I was also reminded of His infinity, His ability to take all the burdens that weighed so heavily on my shoulders into the galaxies of His splendor. He could carry it all for me, so that I could happily rest completely in His bigness.

Nathan may have thought these nights were especially for him, but I know truly that they were intended for my mama heart, to give me some hours in the lovely, shadowy night to be at rest.

CHAPTER 7

Wrestling God

Why Life Is a Full-Contact Sport

NATHAN

I wrung my hands together, palms sweaty. My legs swung restlessly beneath my desk chair as I looked out my bedroom window. The darkening sky seemed to mirror the shadow that had fallen over my consciousness.

For the past few days I had been wrestling with just about the biggest question a twelve-year-old can ask. I felt uneasy and scared as a result, but I knew it was time to confess.

My heart beat faster and faster as I heard footsteps coming down the stairs, headed for my room. I took a deep breath in and tried to prepare myself for what would come next.

There was a gentle knock at my bedroom door.

"Come in," I quavered.

My mother stepped through the door and into my room.

With eyes glued to the floor, I slowly swung my desk chair to face her. Concern filled her bright-blue eyes as she sat down gently on my bed.

"Is everything okay, Nathan?" she asked.

I didn't answer immediately. I decided that the words I had been rehearsing just weren't good enough and began searching my brain for better ones.

Then, finally, I could hold it in no longer. I had to release the pressure no matter what the outcome. So I just blurted it out.

"I have doubts about God."

There was a pregnant silence. I prepared for the worst. Then I quickly shot a glance up to see what damage had been done.

Concern faded into a soft smile as she looked at me.

"Me too," she said.

My brow furrowed as I let her reply sink in.

"You do?"

"Of course. Everyone does, even the strongest of believers."

A comforting warmth crept over me. I wiped my hands on my pants.

"I want to believe in God. It's just I don't always know He's there. What should I do when I feel like that?" I asked.

My mother looked up at the ceiling as if God was sitting there, telling her what to say. Then she looked back at me.

"Keep talking to God. Tell Him your questions and doubts, the things you want to know, and the things you don't understand."

"Really?" I asked.

"Nathan, God is big enough for all your questions, and He wants to hear them all."

As I pondered that, I felt my angst slowly fade away, making room for a brand-new view of this mysterious God I had so many questions about. I learned that day that questions are beautiful and that doubt is a part of being human.

....

My eight-year-old fingers tapped on the hard wooden pew as the pastor of our small church droned on for what seemed like three hours. I was just old enough to start sitting in church with the grown-ups, but my racing mind and restless body disagreed.

My legs swung freely in succession beneath me, and my eyes darted around the sanctuary, searching for something more interesting than what was happening behind the pulpit.

I knew I should be focused on the sermon. I mean, I was eight, old enough to understand some deeper theology. But no matter how hard I tried—and I had tried again and again over the past few weeks—I simply couldn't keep my mind engaged. Every time we reached the ten-minute mark, my mind would wander out of my head and outside, ready to find adventures and build forts.

Suddenly I felt a hand on my leg. I looked up to see my

mom and dad giving me "the look." I quickly shoved my hands beneath my legs and looked at the floor.

Then my dad reached into a bag on the floor and handed my mother a book to hand to me. It looked like a Bible—red pleather cover, golden inscription across the front. But when I gently opened the mysterious book, I was delighted to find pages filled with so much more than just black-and-white words. It was a comic-book Bible!

I began to flip through the brightly colored pages. And page by page, the stories of the Old and New Testaments came to life, igniting my imagination. Then I turned another page, and one particular picture caught my eye.

I remember to this day how powerful that picture was for me. It was the story from the book of Genesis about Jacob wrestling God (see Genesis 32:22-32).

There was a muscled Jacob locked arm in arm with a mysterious figure as they wrestled through the night.

Eventually the man told Jacob to let go.

And Jacob, recognizing his opponent, replied, "I will not let You go until You bless me."

Even at my young age, the story struck me powerfully. I felt an instant kinship with the powerful Jacob—partly because I, too, decided I would one day have muscles as big as his, but also because Jacob seemed larger than life. He wasn't a stranger to trouble. And he fearlessly asked questions beyond his own understanding, even of God.

The implications of that blew me away. Jacob wrestled with God Himself. And instead of being punished or diminished, he received God's blessing. Jacob wasn't blessed in spite of his decision to wrestle God. He was blessed *because* of it.

Some eighteen years later, on a warm day in an apartment in California after a particularly hard month, I sat in front of a computer. The e-mail on the screen contained yet another no. I had faced rejection after rejection in my auditions as an actor. I was having trouble in my relationships. And the hopelessness that comes with having no job swept over me.

Going where I had learned to go in times of darkness, I picked up my phone and called my mom. She could tell from my voice that I was struggling. "What's wrong?" she asked.

I told her I was mad at God, that it felt like He wasn't holding up His end of the deal. In reply there was a soft silence, just like I had heard all those years before. I held my breath and waited. But then, instead of berating me for my lack of faith or making me feel guilty for not trusting enough, Mom simply reminded me of the story I had read all those years ago in my comic-book Bible. She said that fighting God isn't just something we *can* do, but something we *should* do.

"God loves it when you wrestle Him, Nathan," she said. "Because wrestling is a full-contact sport, and God loves it when you are in contact with Him. Maybe He has a bigger view of your life and is willing to do more than you can presently see."

I hung up the phone feeling a little better. None of my problems were fixed, but I had a new perspective on where

I was. I continued to explore my doubts in the coming days and weeks. And interestingly enough, I found myself closer to Him than I ever had been before.

Who would have thought that the secret to growing closer to God was to wrestle Him?

So often we are told to sit down and be good, to fall in line and not question authority. We're given the impression that good and true believers will just smile and nod and accept what we've been told about God.

But simply accepting things has never been my strong suit.

I've always had the kind of mind that questions. Doubts have always tended to bubble up out of my heart and swirl around in my mind, causing me for better or worse to wrestle with the truth. I'm a fighter by nature, and sometimes that has gotten me into trouble.

But I believe God created me this way. He created many of us like that. We were designed to question and doubt. To wrestle Him.

Because just as my mother said, wrestling is a full-contact sport.

And God loves it when we are in contact with Him.

Sally

Dangling my legs over the concrete edge of the unfinished ten-story hotel room, I looked out on a dazzling sunset and let the beauty of it slowly seep into my bruised soul. I had sneaked up to the site of the hotel being constructed down the street from my home after the construction crew was gone. As a teen, I often needed to walk miles and miles to work off the adrenaline that days of disillusionment had built up in me. Growing up in a high school where there were drugs, lots of alcohol, and a "fast" popular crowd meant that I didn't always fit in.

That's not to say I didn't have friends. I ran around with ten girls who regularly spent the night at each other's house. In a way, I was the ringleader who tied them all together— I ran our calendar and arranged places for us to go and houses where we would meet. But oddly enough, even though several of these girls regularly told me, "You are my best friend," I almost always felt alone.

My heart was restless, longing for more, looking for purpose. I often wished someone would take the time to know me—the real me—and then still love me just as I was. Coming from a high-performance family, I did not always feel that kind of unconditional love. My parents loved me a lot, but there was always an emphasis on grades, weight, and looks, and I never felt I measured up. Nothing I did seemed to be enough. Or at least the things I did were not what my mama would have chosen.

I had learned to perform well and to play the part I was taught to play. I'd learned the right "look," the acceptable behavior. But inside I felt a deep hole of emptiness. Despair and longing swept over me every day, and often I felt that no one really saw or cared to pursue the person inside of me.

Those feelings were what brought me to that hotel construction site at sunset.

My parents would have had cardiac arrest if they'd known I had slipped past the Danger—Do Not Enter signs and climbed up ten stories to sit on the edge of the unfinished rooms, feet hanging over the ledge a couple of hundred feet in the air. But this place, where just God and I met alone, was where I could pour out my doubts, my loneliness, my questions, and my pain. This was where I found small bits of reprieve.

Up here, somehow, I could speak out my deepest thoughts. I could be myself with no pretension and no performance. With just God and me watching the pinks, purples, oranges wash across the horizon in the silence of an abandoned building, somehow I found comfort.

Brushstrokes of dark doubt and shadows of existential anxiety painted the landscape of my mind every day. If anyone could have looked into my soul, that person would have been concerned about my well-being.

Outside, I was a busy teen talking on the phone, speaking of a new crush, going out every night with friends—a picture of happy, carefree youth hurtling toward adulthood. Inside, my heart was clouded with a fog of despair, haunted by persistent loneliness, doubts, and questions.

Observing the many who called themselves Christians but lived ordinary, self-obsessed, burdensome lives, I would ask, "If people *really* knew the God who created this universe, wouldn't their lives be outwardly different—more, better, greater?"

My parents could not fathom what was going on with me. "Why do you have so many questions?" they would ask in annoyance. "Why can't you just be satisfied with life as it is? Why do you persist in challenging every thought, every motive, every philosophy of the world around you? Just give it up."

That just made it worse—the fact that no one could validate me, no one even tried. How I wish someone had been there to look into my eyes, see my troubled soul, and give me time to unload my burdens. If even one adult had listened and given attention to my heart of doubts, I would have felt companionship in my struggles. But no one did.

This was several years before I actually understood who God was, fell in love with the story of Jesus, and allowed His words to bring healing to my heart. But it all began when I was wrestling with the meaning of life alone in an unfinished building, watching the sunset ten stories up. That was when my path began to lead me to Him.

So many years later, when each of my children came to me with deep doubts, I understood. Their pathway was one I had walked, and I knew their need for compassion, sympathy, and support. So I would put aside the screaming demands of my own busyness, listen to their words, and seek to comprehend their soul issues.

I knew from experience that God would be faithful to answer their deepest questions. He is profoundly real, present even in darkness—as Psalm 139:12 tells us, "even the darkness is not dark" to Him. I had learned this for myself. So I could be His hands and voice to encourage my children to keep following hard after Him until they found what they were searching for.

In a world awash with pain, sadness, violence, difficulty, rejection, and hypocrisy, despair and doubt may sometimes be the most honest responses we can give. Yet God lives here still. I know that from experience too.

As we light candles of faith in the darkness that surrounds us, as we reach out to hold hands through our days and extend love to hurting hearts, we can become the assurance that doubting hearts need to know they are not alone. Through us, God is redeeming life, creating beauty, loving the unlovely, and bringing hope to the lost souls. And He wants us to develop eyes that can see inside another's heart instead of just looking on the outside. Extending sympathy and compassion and taking time to listen can make a massive difference in the life of someone who is struggling with doubt and despair in the lonely recesses of his or her soul.

God's existence does not diminish just because we have doubts. His transcendence swallows up the darkness; He dances through our world to bring life and light into longing hearts who strain to know Him. And we become His agents when we hold the hands of others and offer our help and affection, when we extend words of compassion and mercy, and when we offer to carry them in our hope when they can't find any of their own.

CHAPTER 8

Different Drumming

....

Embracing the Songs of Our Hearts

NATHAN

I loved screamo music.

If you don't know what that is, it's a genre of music—some would argue otherwise—that features raging guitars, heavy drums, and, yes, screaming vocals.

I can only imagine what my mother must have thought when she caught snippets of the intense, sometimes terrifying, *boom-boom-boom*s and *roaaar*s that flowed through my headphones. But as a teenager with mental illness, I felt like I'd found music that finally understood me.

I would cruise Christian music channels and, trying to be

the good Christian kid, I would listen to what I found there. But I usually found an impossible disconnect between the angst I felt inside and the messages being given. It seemed to me that most of the "uplifting" music only wanted to talk about good things. It spun life in a way that either tried to "fix" me or ignored the pain I was feeling altogether.

But when I pushed Play on *my* music, the screamo sound simply echoed the chaos and frustration I felt, allowing me to exorcise and slowly release my deep frustrations.

Here's the thing about living with severe anxiety, depression, OCD, or any other mental illness or personality trait: It's not something you choose.

You didn't invite it over and it just outstayed its welcome.

You didn't somehow catch it on your way to work and can knock it out with a couple of aspirin and a good nap.

It isn't a switch that you turn on and can easily shut off.

For some (like me) it's something you are born with. For others it happens as a result of the family you were born into or circumstances that happened to you that you had little or no control over.

But no matter how you got it, it isn't a choice.

Instead it's an every-minute, every-second lens through which you see the world. It's like being color-blind. You can try and try to see the world like the people around you do, but try as you might, you simply cannot. So you're fated to live with a perspective you are powerless to change.

Where the rest of the world sees a crosswalk, you see almost certain death.

Where the rest of the world sees a bright sunny day, you see a gauntlet to run.

Where most people see a dollar bill, you see only the contaminating bacteria from the thousands of thousands of dirty hands that have already held it.

Where they see a crowded room, you see an army of foes ready to attack.

Whatever you see, it's something that separates you from the crowd, otherwising you, until you wonder if you are seeing a completely different world than everyone else.

As a kid, I used to wonder if everyone saw colors differently, if what I might know as red would look like yellow to you.

Later I began wondering if everyone saw the world differently.

Slowly I came to think that maybe it was just me.

....

I dropped my backpack on the floor with a thud as my full weight fell onto the bed in my basement room. It had been a terrible day by a sixteen-year-old's standards.

Recently I had enrolled in classes at the local high school, hoping I could spend more time with friends I had met at church. But being the six-foot-three, two-hundred-pound, homeschooled new kid with a lisp didn't exactly help me fit in.

It had been one of those days where strike after strike had beaten me down, and by the time I made it home and fell into my room, I had nothing left. Earlier that day a teacher had scolded me for not following the "rules" on a creative project, humiliating me in front of the class. Then a couple of the popular kids had yelled, "Gay!" as I passed by in the hallway, their laughs echoing down the hall.

That had been just the beginning. And while I tried my best to shrug off the darts the day had landed in my skin, the wounds still stung, festering into blisters on my soul. By the time I was safely back in my room, all I could manage to do was shove my headphones on and push Play.

The music started with a heavy beat, soaring electric guitars, screaming vocals. Just what I needed.

I felt my heart beat faster and my hands begin to tap to the rhythm. I let the song encircle me as I found solace the best way I could. As the music thumped into my soul, I got up and walked to the beat-up drum set that I had bought from a friend for a hundred dollars. Music still roaring in my headphones, I picked up my sticks and began to play along. Beat after beat, I slammed my sticks into the drums, slowly releasing all the frustration that came with growing up me.

I did this almost every day, playing with such ferocity that often I would break sticks. Even the metal cymbals would sometimes crack beneath the power of my strikes. I would play until my heart was satisfied, until the voices in my head were silent, until my hands bled. The drums let me pour everything I had into the song I was hearing.

I can only imagine what my family must have thought as the noise boomed through the walls of our house, having no context for the banging. But even though they couldn't hear the song I heard, they loved me enough to let me dance to its beat.

....

Fast-forward ten years. I was now a twenty-six-year-old man making his way in the world by way of New York. As I stepped outside one cool September evening, escaping the pile of grown-up tasks and the four small walls of my studio apartment, I felt the sinking sun touch my face as a gentle wind funneled down the busy street.

I had moved to the city two months earlier, chasing a dream. As with any move, the reality proved very different from the pictures in my head. I loved New York, the energy and possibility that lay around every corner. But having just emerged from one of the hardest years of my life and headed to a new metropolis with no friends, no job, and just a box of clothes and a bottle of pills, I also faced some unavoidable angst. Tired of being an adult for the day, I now hoped to find some relief on the streets of New York.

The hustle and bustle of the Upper West Side greeted me as person after person passed by the door of my building, each with his or her own set of worries, concerns, and goals.

But not me. Not at this moment. I had decided to leave mine inside.

I reached into my pocket and pulled out my MP3 player. I pushed Shuffle and put in my earbuds. And there it was again—my music. The same soaring guitars, pounding drums, and larger-than-life screaming vocals, working their way into my soul and echoing my emotions. I began to walk, and again I could feel the beat in my hands. And as the music flowed into my ears and through me, I picked up my air instruments and played along.

I beat the drums to the beat and nailed every guitar solo.

As I walked, I got some strange looks from passersby, and I can only imagine what they must have been thinking as a towering adult man rocked out on the streets of New York. But the music wasn't for them. It was my song to dance to, so I did—but perhaps if they could've heard it, they would've rocked out too.

I had other songs now too. As I grew up I'd learned to channel my frustration beyond listening and drumming. I'd learned guitar and a little piano and found solace in writing songs that could both express and ease what I was feeling. All of them were unique to me, the result of the unique way I was made to experience the world. Each individual piece was a stanza in the song I was learning to live.

Each of us has a song God has placed inside of us—one that's unique, unlike anyone else's. We may try to ignore our songs, straining to hear and dance to others that look more inviting or socially acceptable. But on and on our song will play, always inviting us back to move to our own music.

As someone who has always felt different, I grew up wondering if there was something wrong with my song. To others it often sounded loud, chaotic, strange—if they could hear it at all. It wasn't until I realized that God had written a piece for only me that I understood I wasn't supposed to be dancing to anyone else's music. It wasn't until I fully embraced the song God had put on my heart that I was able to live and move the way He had designed me.

And yes, it's still hard when I get stares and condescending looks. There are times when I wish I had a different song. But that doesn't happen nearly so often now.

When you realize your song was divinely written for you, your audience suddenly becomes that of One.

And then you can dance to the music only you were made to hear.

Sally

After more than six decades on this planet, I have come to know myself pretty well. I am an idealist, an ENFP on the Myers-Briggs Type Indicator.[5] As such I have a very strong commitment to life as it should be. Relationships should be close and loving. Home life should be peaceful and nurturing. Education should be rigorous and focused on helping children and adults live into their potential. Food should be as natural as it can be, preferably organic. Christians should be the most loving, generous, excellent people on earth. And children should respect their parents and move steadily toward adulthood and self-discipline, growing in civility—whoops!

Living with Nathan challenged all of these "shoulds" and more on a regular basis. My other unique children challenged them too, but Nathan was much more obvious in his differences. Again and again through the years, I would find myself surprised and frustrated when he found yet another way to thwart my vision for what I thought our lives should be. Nathan boomed through life. He was always a whirlwind of activity, strongly opinionated and usually *loud*.

When he was three, I took the kids to a craft fair held in a hot, crowded gymnasium. It felt like a steam bath in there. Within minutes, sweat was rolling down Nathan's face.

"Let me take your jacket off, sweetie. You won't be so hot."

"No!" Nathan twisted away from me and emphatically announced, "This shirt you put on me embawasses me!"

Yes, he was like that at three. Articulate. Argumentative. And did I mention *loud*?

His opinions started early and were usually different from Clay's and mine. He had strong preferences in almost every area—clothing, music, toys, cartoons—and he wasn't one to acquiesce graciously when thwarted. Throughout his childhood and teen years, Nathan often acted out in ways that embarrassed me or the other kids. He couldn't *not* argue with authorities—at church, in classes, or in other activities.

To make matters worse, through all those years, very few people either understood his issues or would listen to me when I would try to find help for either him or me. I often found myself baffled and frustrated as I sought to understand why Nathan seemed so out of reach of my normal mama training and affection.

The advice I got from others rarely proved helpful.

I found that most people wanted to minimize the issues I dealt with on a daily basis:

- "Nathan's just being a boy! You're making too much of his differences. He will grow out of this."
- "Oh, my kids are OCD too. They always want their socks to match. You shouldn't make such a big deal out of it."

Or they offered simplistic, judgmental, and profoundly unhelpful fixes:

- "You need to spank him more."
- "What are you feeding him? You need to change his diet."
- "His strong will and loudness is sin. You need to confront him and control his behavior."
- "That loud music is demonic and will lead him to rebellion."

Hammering my insecurity, the blows of people's words and judgments left wounds on my heart, too. Sometimes the worst thing you can do to people is to minimize their issues and offer pat answers—and I received plenty of those. Many times I just felt a need for someone to listen, to sympathize, to understand, and to pray. Instead, I often felt alone as I struggled to relate to Nathan in a way that gave him structure and guidance without generating more confrontation or conflict. Very few people seemed to understand or even *try* to understand what life was like for us. But repeatedly I felt the silent criticism of others because of my inability to "make him behave."

Being the parent who stayed home with the kids (I worked from a tiny office space in our various homes) probably increased that feeling of isolation. So did being the more emotionally driven parent, with a deep desire to empathize and understand Nathan's mysterious struggles. I was the only one engaged all day long with Nathan, and that was often a lonely place to be.

I want to add that this was a time when there were fewer resources available for parents of different children and a lot more suspicion about mental-health challenges. Information was hard to come by, and even doctors knew less about these areas. I am thankful to know that a lot of this has changed. Today it is much easier for parents to educate themselves and find help in the form of support groups, books, online resources, and professionals who can offer insight. Even the public in general is better informed, though much is still misunderstood. So things are better, and we hope this book can be a supportive resource as well.

....

As an extrovert with OCD, Nathan said everything that came into his head, told everyone what he thought, and was almost always bigger than life in the way he expressed himself. One of my other kids described it this way: "Nathan says what all of us think but don't say, so he is always the one who gets in trouble." All of us in our family got used to the "talks" I would have to have with Nathan's teachers—music, art, speech, Sunday school—tennis coaches, and other adults who interacted with him. Often these meetings were followed by the ones the other kids all had to hear in the car afterward when I attempted to explain to Nathan why his behavior was unacceptable. (My kids called these the Nathan Lectures, though they all got their fair share.)

I can understand why Nathan was difficult for teachers and others in authority to handle. Our family lived with him every day, and we found it difficult too. But we did find ourselves longing for more empathy and understanding. We found that public arenas had little margin to give grace to the exceptions like Nathan.

Sadly, we found this was just as true within the Christian community as outside it. Sometimes it was worse. Raising my children in Christian circles meant I was always acutely aware of what was acceptable, what was not acceptable—and what my family, especially Nathan, was doing that fell into the *not*-acceptable category. Perhaps we all live in a private world of wanting to be freer of outside peer pressure and expectations, but we stuff our thoughts, fearful of being criticized. I know that was true of me.

Looking back, I believe a lot of what we experienced as judgmentalism or simply indifference grew out of a profound misunderstanding of and lack of experience with mental illness. And sadly, this seems to persist despite the greater availability of information today.

Recently a timid woman wearing a fearful expression came close to me after a conference and whispered, "Is your son *really* OCD, or does he just have strong preferences?" She had a clinically OCD child and wanted to know if it was a reality that influenced all the moments of our days, as her child's behavior did. She had talked to too many friends who glibly said, "Oh, all of us are a little OCD."

I encounter this often to this day. People who have strong opinions or preferences or who like things orderly will assume (or joke) that they have OCD. But personality differences or tidy tendencies do not determine a clinical OCD profile. OCD involves recurring brain impulses that are not easily stopped. People with this disorder feel they must obey their repetitive, often irrational thoughts and feelings before they can move forward or take the next step in life. We're talking about washing one's hands ten times in a row to be sure they are clean instead of just being a person who prefers clean hands and washes them before meals.

Nathan's OCD, we would eventually learn, was complicated by a cluster of other clinical issues as well. He wasn't *trying* to be difficult. He really *was* different in fundamental ways that required different treatment and lots and lots of grace—both for him and for us.

Until you have had a child with a severe mental or emotional difference—OCD, autism, clinical depression, PTSD, or others—you just don't know how constant the disruption can be every day, all the time. So it's all too easy to assume that the attitudes and outbursts that characterize life with these mysterious children are just the result of a bad attitude, a lack of training, or poor parenting in general.

To complicate matters, children who are undisciplined, unloved, abused, or traumatized can exhibit some of the same attributes and behaviors, so diagnosing children's issues is a complex pursuit. In my mind, that's even more reason to extend grace wherever possible and strive for understanding instead of making assumptions.

I have to admit that even I, Nathan's confessor through almost thirty years, the one he tells everything—and I mean everything!—am still often surprised by his vehement response when I have unknowingly violated an area of his OCD. The offenses that accost him in life vary and change, and I cannot always conceive or anticipate what is going to bother him. Nathan and I are alike in many ways, and we embrace the same values, the same faith. Yet his thinking patterns often are totally out of my ballpark of understanding.

Part of my learning to deal with him was to accept the fact that (1) I would never totally understand him or know how to respond to him, but that (2) that was okay! Carrying guilt for being unable to anticipate all his needs would just add more burden to our lives. An emotional backpack loaded with feelings of inadequacy, guilt, and failure can perilously slow us down or even stop progress entirely.

....

"They got that from you!"

Clay and I have often jokingly pointed our fingers at each other and made that claim when our children were misbehaving. And it's true that we both have our issues, including lots of baggage from dysfunctions in childhood. But I am pretty sure Nathan did get a lot of his issues from my side of the family.

I have learned that a tendency toward clinical OCD and other mental illnesses can be hereditary and often affects more than one member of a family. Three of our four children have been diagnosed with clinical OCD, though only two have it severely. And as I have mentioned, I was a bit of a "wild child" myself—passionate, determined, and no doubt difficult for adults to understand and deal with.

The most quoted story about my childhood involves a time when my grandmother gave my two brothers cowboy hats, guns, and holsters for Christmas and gave me a doll. I threw the doll across the room, tackled one unsuspecting brother, and screamed, "I want to be a cowboy too. Give me your guns!"

I don't feel bad about that one, even if it did embarrass my mom and earn me a stern correction. What self-respecting adventurer wouldn't want to be included in being a hero? But as I grew, I did struggle a lot with feeling like I was too much for most people and unacceptable to them. As a result, I have felt lonely and different most of my life, even when surrounded by many friends. Often I wondered what was wrong with me. My mother's questions were my questions too. Why couldn't I just be like everybody else?

But I have a different perspective these days, partly because of my experience with Nathan. These days I'm inclined to look at those differences—yes, even the ones that made things difficult for everyone—as gifts.

What if my extreme passion and idealism was exactly what God gave me so that I could speak to thousands at a time without being daunted?

What if all that "too much" energy is what enables me to travel twenty-five weekends a year to speak to women all over the world?

What if my very outside-the-box personality suited me for the work God created me to do—including being Nathan's mother?

At the very least, my experience of feeling misunderstood helped me to understand Nathan a little better, to be his advocate, and to train him more effectively. Perhaps because I had felt the deep sting of rejection, I had more of a desire to reach Nathan's heart with acceptance and appreciation, to help him discover his unique, God-given music and dance to it in a way that blessed the world around him.

There are profound ways that I find joy today in being Nathan's close friend. We are bold together, loving to take risks, enjoying life to the fullest, making fun memories as pals. We discuss ideals with passionate seriousness and laugh often over people, dogs, Internet clips, and life in general.

In many ways I find him a soul mate, a match for some of the deepest areas of my heart. But this friendship took many years to develop—many years of listening, observing, experimenting, and trying to understand as Nathan grew from an outside-the-box boy into a complex, interesting, amazing young man.

If Clay and I had looked at Nathan's disabilities and measured the possibilities of his life by what he couldn't do, then we would indeed have limited his life and doomed him to failure. But God eventually gave us the faith to believe that He had a special plan for Nathan's life—that who he was, as he was, could bring great glory to the heavenly Father who created him. So we sought out opportunities for Nathan to be successful and grow and feel accomplished.

One of the truths we came to eventually as a couple and as a family was that Nathan was (and indeed all of our children were) an essential part of the particular story that God wanted us to live out, the place we could best glorify Him. There was never going to be a magic bullet that would take all Nathan's problems away, no advice or childhood discipline book or medication that would provide instant healing, no formula that would remove all the mysterious and demanding stresses he brought our way.

We had to accept Nathan with God's unconditional love—just as he was. We had to accept his mysterious issues as God's perfect will for us and then work within those parameters to guide and train him effectively.

So I tried to respond to Nathan's constant questions and

arguments at the dinner table by listening for the truth of his thinking and correcting him gently. "You need to teach your lips how to be persuasive," I would say. "You have a profound way of thinking, but you will lose your audience if you attack them. How could you have said that with more appeal?" (Yes, we did speak to our young children as though they were adults and could understand our mature thinking.)

....

I have always told my children that they might as well decide to embrace God's will for their lives right where they are and engage in the present moment with as much faith and wisdom and skill as they can, because their circumstances are not going to miraculously change.

Today—this day, not tomorrow, not yesterday—is the day the Lord has made. We must learn to rejoice and be glad in this particular set of circumstances.

If we accept the puzzle we have been given and ask, "What can I learn at this juncture, God? How should I be humble and glorify You in this place?" then we will become stronger, developing muscles of faith, wisdom, humility, and understanding. Contentment and peace come by releasing our expectations and accepting our specific, "right now" circumstances as a place where we can learn to grow and flourish.

For most of us, of course, learning this lesson is a very slow process. (That may be doubly true for idealists like me.) First we expect our children, marriage, work, or ministry to be rosy. Our minds are full of the vision of what our lives can be—flourishing and productive like a beautiful garden.

But then we begin to see the thorns and pests in the gardens of our lives, and we can easily become overwhelmed. The work of pulling the weeds of sin and immaturity, keeping out the insects of bad attitudes in our own lives, and protecting the growth from outside influences and disasters demands so much of us. And many of us have not been trained or prepared for such a long process.

So many worldly voices promise us a secret formula to make life work better: Give the responsibility of our children, home, or family to others. Pay someone else to deal with the mess. Hire a professional gardener—let someone else do the work.

Finally we get it through our heads that making this garden of our lives productive is going to take a lot of work, year after endless year. Then we either make a decision of the will to do the hard work that needs to be done or we give up and allow the weeds and pests to take over.

The process of living with a child who creates conflict daily and often affects the family atmosphere is challenging to each person in the family. We had to give our other children opportunities to express their irritation, to verbalize their frustration, and to feel that we understood their struggle. We never pretended that Nathan was not hard to live with. It took many years of personal growth for Clay and me to learn patience, to extend sympathy, to choose love and appreciation for differences. So we had to extend the same grace and understanding for our other children as they grew from frustration to patience and understanding for Nathan's issues.

As a family, we told our other children, our message was clear: "If it is God's will for Daddy and me to have Nathan as our child (or you with your issues), it is God's will for you to have Nathan as your brother. All of you are what make up the design of our family.

"Our family will always be one for all and all for one. That means Nathan has to learn to be honoring to you and committed to you in your needs. It also means you need to be as faithful as you know how in accepting what it means to be a committed sibling to him and to each other. All of us have a family puzzle unique to us that we have to learn to put together with acceptance and grace."

It wasn't always easy. In fact, it was often far from easy. As we have told our children a thousand times, life in a fallen world is not fair. But little by little, step by step—even through dark times that seemed overwhelming—we saw God faithfully work in our lives. Clay and I rejoiced to see our children growing in love for one another as they practiced extending kindness and sympathy.

It has taken a lifetime of patiently cultivating the right values, watering them with love, and then watching them grow to fruition. But I have been gratified to watch all our children grow their commitment to always love each other, to be loyal to one another, and to extend grace to one another.

To me that's true satisfaction.

....

Having Nathan tested by local educational and psychological gurus did give us some helpful insight into his issues. One woman explained to me that Nathan's mind took in everything that was in our world all at the same time. Most people have a filter that allows them to choose what they will allow their brain to focus on. But Nathan's brain was always taking in every sensory stimulus that bombarded him. This meant that concentrating on one thing was very challenging for him. It also meant that he perceived and reacted to things that most of us were not even aware of in the moment. Noises, sights, colors, voices, instruction, and thoughts in his own head—all were firing at once, with no natural filter. Living this way was exhausting for him, and agitation was a natural reaction.

Once I understood this, I began to find ways to help Nathan calm down so he could learn and grow. I noticed, for instance, that vigorous activity seemed to help him concentrate better. So before our reading times, I would have him run around the house a few times or throw the ball for the dog.

Loud, rhythmic music also seemed to make him happy and help him settle, so we gave him headphones and a little MP3 player so he could rock out and settle himself down. We encouraged him to play the drums because banging hard along with his music seemed to calm him down. (Yes, I did buy myself multiple sets of earplugs.)

As for the screamo music, I am not a fan. But through the years we found we had to draw our lines in the sand for the issues that were not negotiable and be flexible in others. Music was an area where we chose to be flexible. And of course there were those who wanted to be sure to tell us that Nathan's music was demon possessed and that he would lose his faith if he listened to it.

It wasn't, and he didn't.

But helping Nathan involved more than just finding ways for him to calm down. I also wanted to discover what his strengths were and help him excel in those areas. For instance, homeschooling turned out to be the best place for him to flourish educationally.

Working with Nathan one-on-one, I could make realistic goals for him, train him in godly character little by little, and engage him in what captured his imagination and interest at his own pace, within the bounds of his personality quirks. This would not have been possible in a traditional classroom. Though challenging for me, homeschooling gave him a place where he was not ostracized all the time for his behavior. At home he was freer to be himself without the constant correction of his peers and authorities.

I chose to homeschool all my children and loved it even more than I ever thought I would. We all enjoyed the same stories and shared the same engaged thoughts as we studied great people together. And the kids were able to play wild and free for hours at a time—acting out stories, creating imaginative projects, running, exploring, and pondering life outdoors. As they grew older, we supplemented their education with extracurricular activities and specialized classes arranged through our local homeschooling support groups, which offered instruction in a "cottage school" on a limited weekly basis.

As I look back, I think having his own gang of siblings around him all day every day helped Nathan feel like he had a people to belong to and a place to belong. As an extrovert, he loves people, but being with large groups can aggravate his sense of being different. Being part of our home gang, who knew him well and (usually) accepted him as he was, gave him that sense of not being alone without having to face a lot of outside surprises that might agitate his OCD.

One of our goals for all our children, but especially Nathan, was to find areas where they could excel, develop skill sets suited to their personalities, and find places where they could thrive. Nathan loved physical activity and was very well coordinated, so he was a natural for sports, but teamwork did not come easy to him. Tennis seemed a good choice for him because it's a more individual sport. For some years, therefore, we invested in tennis lessons and found a small tennis team so he could play occasionally in competitions and learn teamwork without the pressure of a big-team activity.

Nathan was also a natural performer who loved the adrenaline rush of playing to audiences, so we looked for ways to help him develop his abilities in these areas. As he grew, for instance, he loved juggling and sleight-of-hand tricks.

So Clay took him to national conferences where big-stage illusionists performed and showed youth how to present the gospel through this medium. For a while Nathan and a friend performed birthday-party magic shows where they presented the gospel at the end. And as he grew older, we occasionally had him speak at conferences and marveled at the ease with which he addressed large audiences. No wonder he eventually decided to become an actor and then a filmmaker.

....

Having his own places to excel and to engage apart from the other children in our family gave Nathan his own sense of self-confidence and self-actualization. Working at his own pace, within his own skill set, where his heart would be engaged helped him believe that God could use him to make a difference in the world.

But I had to change my own tune, so to speak, for that to happen.

I had to make my peace with drumbeats pounding through the house at all hours when I have would preferred some soothing Celtic tunes.

I needed to go outside and walk and run with Nathan when I would rather sit on the porch with a cup of tea.

I needed to be intentional about surrounding him with stories that delighted his heart and supported his dreams of being a hero.

I had to seek out ways for him to shine, to discover his personal song and then share it with the world.

As I tried to do all these things, I sensed God cultivating a vision for Nathan in my heart. Instead of comparing him to others, even to my other children, I began to appreciate his uniqueness—his passion about what he loved, the ways he engaged in stories, and how much he loved heroes and wanted to be one.

As a matter of fact, now that I know Nathan as an adult, I love the man he has grown to be. I enjoy his outside-the-box thinking, his passion for what he does, and his engaged, opinionated personality. I appreciate his strength and the perseverance that kept him through so many days of struggle. And I admire his willingness to trust God for big dreams beyond what he could ever do for himself, to risk creating stories that might inspire others when most people told him it was impossible to make it in the entertainment industry.

It's a great gift to be able to say that you not only love your child, but you respect him too. I thank God that I can say that about my Nathan. And I honestly believe the world needs to catch the rhythm of the song he is singing.

CHAPTER 9

A Place to Belong

A Home Base for Thriving

NATHAN

My neck filled with warmth as I felt the frustration rising. My jaw clenched and my muscles tightened. All around me I could feel the eyes of the class, but I was looking dead ahead at an exasperated teacher—all because of one tiny question: "Why?"

An hour earlier when the class began, there had been no malice in my heart. And if you had told me that in a short while I would be confronted by a teacher who was so exasperated that she resorted to yelling, I wouldn't have believed you.

The class was at our church. We were studying a book

about God, and through the course I'd begun to have more and more questions that no one else in class seemed to have. Me being me, I'd felt I needed to say something. So every time I found what looked like an inconsistency or logical error, I had quickly jumped in to state my thoughts.

I could see the young teacher's growing frustration with every passing comment I dropped. But truth was truth, and I felt it was my duty to say something.

I had no intention of being disruptive. But I could feel all the questions dropping in my mind like bullets, and my hand would fly up with each new one. Eventually I was given a dismissive "just because" answer I felt was unsatisfactory. So before the teacher even had time to take a breath, I asked why. Then I did it again and again until finally, out of what I thought was nowhere, I found myself on the receiving end of a frustrated, yelling teacher.

Her eyes were wide and her mouth ajar as she stared at me, most likely a bit surprised at her own reaction. I was surprised, too, though in all honesty, this wasn't the first time I had pushed a teacher, parent, or sibling to the limit.

"Nathan, please stay after class."

My stomach dropped inside of me, and I could feel an angry sob behind my eyes that I refused to let out. How was this happening again? I wasn't trying to be bad; I was trying to learn. And I was right. Couldn't she see that?

"Class dismissed," she said, finally breaking her stare. One by one the other kids silently shuffled out, and passing me on their way out the door, I could feel their stares pierce into my bruised being. Then I was left alone with the teacher.

A heavy silence hung in the air as she walked to her desk and began packing her things into a bag, no doubt searching for the words to address me. Then, pausing, she turned around and told me I needed to stop disrupting class with my questions. I told her I wasn't trying to disrupt the class, but that if she said something I thought was unclear, I needed to ask about it.

I just wanted to know the truth. Why was that such a problem for her?

....

My footsteps were heavy as I walked through the front door of my home, sat down hard, and slumped onto the living room couch. What a day!

Without warning, our current golden retriever, Kelsey, appeared out of nowhere and attacked me with a barrage of licks and paws, welcoming me home. In the next room I heard the piano playing loudly as Joel played a song from *Les Misérables* while Sarah and Joy sang along. Stepping into the kitchen, I was greeted with the inviting aromas of fresh bread and simmering soup. Mom moved around the kitchen, pulling the last bits of the evening meal together.

My heart was still tired, but the warmth of home was gently melting the ice from the day.

"Welcome home, my Nathan." Mom smiled as she washed her hands.

"Thanks," I managed weakly.

"Why don't you sit down? We're almost ready."

I slowly walked to the dining room as the sounds, smells, and sights of home wrapped themselves around me.

One by one the family found their seats around our over-sized table. The candles were lit, the prayer was said, and we began. But I could still feel the ache in my heart from being caught off guard and admonished for what I believed to be "just my personality."

Little by little as the evening wore on, while the loved ones around me talked, sang, and chimed in, I began to find myself again. Eventually I jumped into the conversation, adding my voice to the five others. I challenged thoughts and engaged in discussion and even asked questions like "Why?" And this time my questions were met with nothing but more friendly discussion. By the time dinner was over I had finally relaxed. It felt so good to be back in the place where I was allowed to be me.

Who we are is important.

But finding where we are allowed to thrive as who we are is just as crucial.

For so much of my life, in so many situations, I have

found friction and angst when I was just being myself, whether it was asking too many questions or being too loud. So often I found myself in places where I didn't feel accepted for who I was.

But no matter where I went or what I did, I always knew that as soon as I opened my front door I would be welcomed home. My family had created a place where I was not only allowed but encouraged to be Nathan, the person God made me to be.

I was not asked to put on a safer, more acceptable personality. I was not asked to be someone I was not. I was simply allowed to be who I was—as I learned to accept and love the ones around me for who they were. Home was truly a safe space put together by my parents and brought to life by my family, who all knew me so well and actually loved me for it.

Unfortunately, not all of us are lucky enough to have a home where we can exist as our full selves without being expected to be someone else. The world is broken, and so are our minds, our families, and our homes.

But I believe there's a place where we can always find the warmth and peace of knowing there's a place for us to exist. We can find it in the presence of our Creator, the One who designed us in the first place, who knows even better than we do who we were made to be, and invites us to participate with Him in bringing His Kingdom to earth.

We can bring to Him all of our flaws and failures and frustrations—all of our ideas and questions. He is our gracious

Maker who always loves us just as we are while growing us into all we can be.

In Him we find our truest and most welcoming home.

Sally

Nathan barreled in the front door, plopped loudly onto the living room couch, and sighed as though the world was coming to an end. "It happened again, Mama. I got in trouble with my big mouth. And this time it was with that friend of yours who teaches my class!"

My stomach did a familiar flip-flop, and a sort of shadow passed over my heart at the thought of his feeling like an outcast *again*. From experience of all of his years growing up, I knew how he argued, but also how he was misunderstood. And I especially knew the heartbreak that comes to a mama who wants everyone to love and understand her different child but finds that few will take the time to invest gentleness, compassion, and affirmation into his heart.

It seemed that most of our personal world did not want to look past Nathan's issues, to truly listen to him and understand his heart, or to take into consideration his real value. Most just wanted to judge his behavior and his outside-the-box way of looking at life, or they saw him as just an inconvenience.

This made me hurt for him—and worry about him a little too.

....

When I was a young woman just out of high school, some-one very close to me killed herself. The suicide note said, "I just wanted someone to take enough time to notice me and tell me I was okay, but they didn't. I just couldn't take the rejection and loneliness anymore."

Understandably, this incident affected me deeply. I often asked myself, *Could I have made a difference if I had called her or reached out more often?*

In our broken world, there is—and will be—much that we cannot understand or control. I have known loving, intentional parents whose children choose a prodigal path. An innocent girl from our church was killed by a stray bullet. Cancer and other illness—including mental illness—have struck down so many. And the tragic reality is that some of our beloved mentally ill or otherwise troubled children, overwhelmed by the pain of being different, choose to end their story by ending their own lives.

The belief that God is good and that He loves us is our foundation to stand on in times of deep heart and soul test-ing. But faith does not take away the pain and anguish; it does not diminish the unforgettable years of heartbreak and despair. Sometimes we need a lifetime to even begin moving beyond the tragedies that our lives bring.

But that doesn't mean we are helpless in the face of trag-edy or that there is nothing we can do to help. The suicide of that young woman and my experience with other hurting people over the years—including those in my family—taught me the value of stopping to listen to others, trying to understand them, helping them feel seen. Often the memory of this tragedy stops me in my tracks to give those in my life a moment of my time when otherwise I would just get on with my piles of responsibilities.

I grieve for those I meet who have had tragedies in their families and have experienced unmentionable loss. And I have learned from experience that sometimes when people in our lives seem to be doing fine, underneath they are crumbling.

God offers grace to all of us as we fumble and make mistakes along the way. He also brings grace to us when we have given our all and our loved ones or children have still made destructive choices or suffered from misfortune. He does not require us to control our children or friends, much less "fix" them. But he does call us to pay attention, to love others, to be the ones who reach out as consistently as possible.

Learning to look more deeply into the heart of others by asking what was behind their actions was a life lesson that took me many years to learn. By God's grace I was forced to learn it through Nathan. And by God's grace, I can keep on practicing it. I can speak the words of love, comfort, and understanding to those in my life who fight the same battles as I do but who may be unable to articulate their struggles.

Realization dawned on me slowly through the years that because God loved me so dearly and because I had said I would be His girl, committed to Him with my whole life, He gave me the privilege of being Nathan's mother. Nathan was one of the instruments God used to get my attention, to show me I could not live this life without His help, and to teach me where the heart of my ministry would be.

I had a deep desire to become more spiritual, but I had always imagined it would be by accomplishing heroic acts or serving God in some public arena. Yet God wanted me to understand Jesus, our humble servant king. So He used Nathan to show me that my righteousness would be learned not in my public life, but in the hidden life of our home, where no one would see.

My most important ministry would unfold one obedient moment after another as I learned to love and understand and serve those who were closest to me. Nathan or one of my other family members would push my buttons. And I would have to overcome my feelings and practice giving patient answers, to give up my rights one more time.

Walking in the Spirit, not by my flesh, became a reality through years of yielding my feelings and frustration to God and asking Him to give me grace for each moment of my days. As I have told my kids many times, walking in the power of the Holy Spirit often means choosing to be patient and loving when you feel like being impatient and angry. It is the practicing of growing in these areas that grows our spiritual muscle. God was helping me to grow up by living into the specific puzzle of life called Nathan—His gift for me.

....

As I pondered what Nathan must be feeling on a regular basis, I wanted him to know that he (and all who entered this space) had a home where he would always belong. This was his place to fall apart, to refuel, to restore, to be free to be himself even in times of emotional messes.

But learning to create this kind of atmosphere took me years to grow into, seasons to practice. People do not have needs at convenient times, but at the most inopportune moments. So I had to stretch muscles of patience, endurance, sympathy, and compassion day after day to make our home a source of comfort and encouragement to my family, our depressed friends, and myself as well.

My book *The Lifegiving Home: Creating a Place of Belonging and Becoming* (cowritten with my daughter Sarah)[6] grew out of years of seeing how important a sense of place can be to each of us. Home is a place that can hold us and make us feel we belong, a welcoming place where people can come to feel part of a healing community. It is where those who find rejection in the outside world can come to receive unconditional love and acceptance—and then, perhaps, a gentle nudge to become stronger and better.

But cultivating a home that holds people "safe and loved" requires forethought, practice, preparation, and carefully cultivated skills. It requires intentionality of effort (it won't just happen) and also a release of expectations (it will almost never happen just the way we plan!).

I often thought of my role in our home as that of a conductor of God's beautiful music there—planning and directing the details of atmosphere and activity in ways that would convey His love, His mercy, and His grace to all who entered my home.

Cultivating an experience of beauty within our walls was an important part of creating that sense of welcome and belonging. I learned I could create a sense of peace and joy by appealing to the senses in many ways. Crafting delicious meals, planting colorful flowers, playing transcendent music, filling each corner with art and books—all of these sent a stream of life flowing through that soothed irritations and fueled agitated hearts.

We built playgrounds and tree houses in our yards so our children would have places to retreat from the stresses of life. We stored music, movies, games, and art tools for passing time at home happily and enjoying the act of creation. Family feasts, movie nights, and traditions of celebrating life in big and small ways gave us all a sense of having our own gang, our own club, so to speak, so that even through seventeen moves we all felt as though we had a people to belong to.

Nathan especially seemed to bloom when he was home. His spirit soared after time with the family and maybe a game of catch with a golden retriever. He needed a rest from the places where he did not feel he fit in.

....

Not one of us will ever be able to live fully according to our own ideals and heart rules. We are imperfect. It is why we need a Savior. And when God removes our ability to control life, when we are thrust into utter dependence on Him, our lives begin to take shape in His spiritual reality.

As long as we believe we can control life by trying, controlling, manipulating, putting pressure on life, we will live in constant exhaustion. We learn daily of our need for His Spirit to live through us because we are inadequate in ourselves. We learn to give up expectations that life will ever be perfect and to be content in the midst of the chaos.

Many times mamas (and teachers) think and act as though their difficult children are disobeying and thwarting their rules on purpose, with malice in their heart. All children, of course, are sinful and self-centered (like all humans) as well as immature. Parents are given the task of disciplining and training their children so that they can move from immaturity to maturity and become more loving and others-centered in the process.

In the case of special-needs or outside-the-box children, we are required to become even wiser in our interacting and discipline. Intuition and years of experience taught me that Nathan was not always trying to be loud, misbehave in crowds, or walk outside the boundaries when the other kids were walking in bounds. His capacity to conform to expectations was much more limited than that of my other children.

Yet Nathan was infinitely precious to God as he was, and so I learned to treat him as a gift, not a curse. And I am quite sure that I would not have ever learned humility on my own if God had not given me four imperfect children who tested the maturity and limitations of imperfect me every day of their lives.

I trained, instructed, affirmed, encouraged, prayed with, and gave responsibilities to Nathan little by little and led him forward step by step toward godly character and self-control. I learned not to expect the same behavior or maturity from him as from the others. But I also learned from having four children that each of them grew at their own pace. Each had issues throughout their lives, and each matured little by little.

I also realized that each of my children, especially Nathan, needed to feel that the foundation of our relationship was unconditional love and respect for his or her essential self. Home was my primary tool for conveying that truth to them. For Nathan, I wanted it to be a place where he could breathe out the pressure to perform, to conform, to always be "good" when what was defined as good was almost impossible for him, as God made him, to conform to.

I do want to stress that I learned all this over the years, and at no time did I manage it perfectly. No parent does.

Did I ever yell at Nathan? Lose my patience? Answer him sharply? Get frustrated? More times than I ever want to remember. Many times my words were too harsh, my temper too short. Yet I had to learn to forgive myself as God forgave me—over and over again.

It is humbling to be the parent of a child who brings out all of your weaknesses repetitively. But living in guilt for not being perfect will never serve our need to grow stronger.

"Forgetting what lies behind" (Philippians 3:13), we must press on—and press on and press on.

I think the hardest issue for me with Nathan—and actually with all of my children—was that the task of giving and serving was relentless. And I was not an endless source of cheer. When I had to give out on a regular basis without a break, I would eventually become empty and go to a place of darkness and depression.

Eventually I learned to recognize these signs as warnings—my body and heart were speaking to me. In the long-term journey of raising children, especially different children, parents must find ways to refuel emotionally, physically, and mentally.

For me it was essential to take regular breaks away from Nathan. I needed time to catch up on sleep or just have fun and experience pleasure. A meal out, an overnight get-away with a friend, or a dinner date with Clay could work wonders. Saturday morning breakfast at a little French café afforded a desperately needed dose of "me" time. Even time alone in my room with a cup of tea could be a lifesaver.

It took me a little while, but I learned to see my "time-outs" as necessities, not luxuries, and to be vigilant about making room for them in my life. Without them, I found it almost impossible to provide the kind of welcoming, accepting home experience that Nathan and all my children needed.

Cultivating friendship with other women also proved a vital lifeline for me. Scripture advises us to "bear one another's burdens" (Galatians 6:2), and every mother of outside-the-box children needs that. I looked for friends who could listen without judging or offering formulaic advice, who would laugh with me, pray with me, listen to me, and offer practical help—and of course I offered the same to them.

With our frequent moves, finding a group of friends like that could be challenging. Often I had to initiate friendship by inviting others to my house for a meal or a monthly gathering. Today I might join a support group or even look for online friendships with moms who are experiencing what I am.

Evaluating our own needs as women and as mothers and taking steps to get those needs met is a sign of emotional health. I would advise all mamas of different children to make self-care a priority, even seeking out professional counseling if necessary.

Sometimes the time and energy for self-care may seem nonexistent. But making a plan to live a sustainable life amidst the difficulties that come with parenting these children is a necessity to avoid burnout and to make home a source of life for everyone who lives there—including you.

....

Part of Nathan's makeup and personality was that he was a born questioner and an enthusiastic, persistent arguer. His active, restless mind hungered to understand, to probe, to figure things out, even when that meant challenging authority. And part of my job was to gently teach him how to be honest about his questions while being gracious with his words. He needed to learn to show respect and honor to others (including us!), but also to honor and live out who he really was.

When Nathan was a teenager, we had him evaluated according to the Myers-Briggs Type Indicator. Besides all of the issues that described his life, we read that his personality type, ENTP, was the most argumentative, challenging, and extroverted. That made sense—and it showed us that some—though not all—of his issues were personality driven and not a function of his mental illness.

Looking deeper into Nathan's motivations meant I had to understand that he would always have a lawyerly drive to question and get to the bottom of issues. Sometimes when he was growing up, he seemed to be questioning our values and criticizing our deeply held beliefs. But that wasn't his motivation—at least not most of the time. He's just the kind of person who has a hard time with pat answers, incomplete information, dishonesty, or hypocrisy.

Ultimately, Nathan's tendency to question and challenge has served him well. As an adult, he has the highest of ideals. He cares about truth and has dedicated himself to sharing stories that reflect a biblical worldview. He is dedicated to God's values in a world that pours out worldly values and constantly challenges biblical ones.

I have to admit, however, that reaching this understanding and acceptance of Nathan's argumentative tendencies took faith and perseverance on my part—especially since much of the time he was just being ornery. He loved to pick a fight and show off his ability to blast others with his powerful words. So I corrected him constantly for his tendency to run over others.

Teaching all our children to honor others was a priority in our home. I knew if they did not learn to honor Clay and me and other authority figures in their lives, they would probably not learn to honor God and bow their knee to Him in important moments of life. If they did not learn to honor each other and their peers, they would never be able to develop healthy relationships. So I was constantly teaching, correcting, and disciplining around issues of showing respect. But I knew that no one could thrive under constant correction and criticism, so I tried hard to give grace as well.

Knowing when to correct and train, when to overlook, and when to enjoy and praise is a constant balancing act for a parent, but I tried to err on the side of compassion and sympathy with Nathan. These seemed to be the tools that opened Nathan's heart to correction. And these gifts could only be given through personal time invested over and over again.

Nathan always seemed to love talking to me. I can't explain it rationally, but he and I always seemed to click on a friendship level. We sort of "got" each other, which meant that sometimes he would sit and talk to me for thirty minutes at a time without stopping. He always had something to say—that is what often got him into trouble—and he really did need someone to listen with openness. So I had to learn to put aside my expectations of what I could accomplish in a day. This could be quite a sacrifice on my part. Yet I found that when I invested the time to be his trusted, interested friend over and over again—hour by hour, through the years—he did respond to my discipline and training.

Once, after we had spent an hour together in my bedroom with cookies and milk, with Nathan spilling out his thoughts, opinions, jokes, dreams, and serious ponderings, he looked up suddenly and said, "Mama, when you spend time with me, it makes me feel accepted and loved and special. It makes me want to obey you. But when you are too busy to spend time with me, I will do whatever I need to do to get your attention."

Lesson learned! Close relationships and effective mentoring require that we take the necessary time to really see and hear those under our care and in our realm of friendship. Compassion, understanding, and patience drive the effectiveness of our influence. If we desire for our children to love the God we serve and embrace our messages wholeheartedly, we must invest in their lives.

Were there times when I needed a break from Nathan's need for attention and his tendency to argue about *everything*? Absolutely—especially when they happened at dinner.

We ate meals together every night, and as I have indicated in another chapter, our dinner-table conversations could be almost raucous. Often the table seemed to want to lift off the floor from the wild discussions that ensued. And more times than not, my argumentative Nathan was the instigator.

I would dream of a peaceful, easy, no-quarreling meal. But then someone would innocently bring up a subject, and before I knew it, Nathan would be correcting that person and arguing with him or her. Often he was right in his thinking. When he wasn't, he was still insistent.

Quiet evenings were rare for us.

Clay had his own predisposition to jump in with the arguments—not only because he wanted to refine the kids' thinking skills, but also just because of his personality. He loved an "iron sharpens iron" interaction, while I tended to prefer quiet and peaceful conversation. Conflict pretty much drives me crazy. So I would find myself admonishing the whole family again and again. "We *will* speak with grace to one another! We *will* affirm the other one's thoughts. If you choose to create unnecessary contention, you are choosing to eat alone. It's your decision."

It usually worked—for a while. Then, before we knew it, the discussions would start again. But repeating this pattern again and again did teach my children something about getting along with others and using their words well and kindly. I think there are times when all of us moms think our children are not learning anything from our training. But I have lived to see that they were indeed listening. It just took a while for the seeds to grow.

In the meantime, little Joy grew as tired of the arguing as I did. "Mama, do we have to sit at the table one more night and listen to those teenagers argue?" Joy would wrinkle her nose and furrow her eyebrows all at once. "They make me so tired. Can't we ever just eat a meal and have a nice time together? I get so tired when they talk and talk!"

If I as a mom needed a break once in a while, I could understand that our innocent little girl, who just wanted to play, pretend, and live in a happy world, felt it acutely. "Why don't we all eat together on the deck outside," I told her. "And after we're finished, while everyone is still talking, you and I can go for a little walk."

We did not have conflict every night, of course. And I did not correct every single night because I recognized that discussion and debate were part of our family culture. (We called it "talking Torah.")

And over time I could see that these very dinner-table discussions that wore me out shaped all of our children into thinkers, writers, and message makers. The constant challenges sharpened their thinking skills and their ability to reason with others.

Even Joy eventually came to appreciate the rousing arguments that took place most evenings around our table. After joining the debate team in her freshman year of college, she competed in debate tournaments all over the United States, eventually taking first place with her partner in the national tournament. When I congratulated her on this great news, she said, "Mom, people have asked me about my ability to think on my feet and make such strong arguments in our cases. And you know what? I think those years and years of discussions at our dinner table sharpened my mind. So I guess I need to thank Nathan for that. Who'd have ever thought God would use him and the others kids to teach me how to think well? That's really funny!"

....

There is much that we can do to shape our home environments, to make home a haven of peace and acceptance for each person who lives there. But creating a welcoming home also includes the choice to accept the unique design of our families and the limitations of each family member. We have to learn to lean into life as something beautiful even if it is not exactly what we expected. Trusting that God works all things together for the good despite the challenges we face is a gift of worship we give to God. Acceptance with humility must eventually come to each of us if we are to please God and not always fight against the limitations of our own family pattern.

If Nathan had grown up in a home where he was constantly put down and corrected, I think the oxygen of God's love would have been strangled from his heart, which needed a wide berth of unconditional acceptance. Love is the food our hearts need to grow, and so I had to figure out a way to give it in a way he could feel.

Having a space to be himself gave Nathan the ability to grow into the young man he is today, one who deeply values integrity, clear thinking, and truth in every area of life. It is from this grid that he is writing books and screenplays and giving his passion to being a message maker to his generation about God's light and goodness.

We all have times when we're driven to ask God, "Why?" about some aspect of our lives. Why would He allow this conflict, difficulty, challenge, or stress to enter our lives? And I've sometimes wondered why God would give me a child like Nathan, who was hard to handle and pushed my buttons almost every day.

I still don't know all the answers, of course, but I'm beginning to see some of the ways God used my precious ones to help me grow.

As I practiced patience and grace through the years, I began to appreciate how patient and generous God was toward me.

As I sought to understand Nathan's true motivations, the heart behind the questions and the conflicts, I learned to look beyond the surface behavior of those who came my way. I also learned to empathize more with those who were downhearted, discouraged, and guilt ridden, who struggled with feelings of inadequacy.

And in the end, giving up my expectations—opening my hands to release the hold I had on what I thought life should be—gave me the peace I needed, even amidst the conflict and the arguments. Grace became the oxygen of life to me, and breathed in the everyday joy of being fully at home in my life, surrounded by those I loved.

Voices of Darkness, Voices of Truth

······························

The Tricky Journey toward Maturity

NATHAN

I looked out through my window into the black of another Colorado night. I sometimes kept the window open even in the winter because I liked feeling the rush of cold air across my face as I snuggled up under my covers and fell asleep.

But that night, like so many nights speckled through my short life, there was no sleep to be found. Try as I might, every time I closed my eyes I felt only a heavy burden that lay on my chest like a rock, slowly stealing my breath.

I had tried putting on worship music, hoping to drown out the noise of my mind with something good. But nothing could match the volume of the condemning monologues in my head.

Typically my obsessions revolved around the sense that my body wasn't clean or that my room was contaminated. But tonight the dark encompassing thoughts, the voices of condemnation, arose from a deeper place. They came in the form of guilt—something I had never dealt well with in a real and serious way before. I had done something I couldn't take back, something that at the time I felt was almost unforgivable. And there could be no stepping back from the ledge because I had already hurled myself off of it.

Earlier that night my family had planned an outing to dinner and our local Borders bookstore. As a typical (in some ways) fifteen-year-old young man, I had perused the comic books for a bit, but then had decided to keep on exploring for something new to capture my attention.

That's when I found myself in the photography section.

Having a hard time with long pages of words, I often found myself drawn to visually captivating images. So I thought this would be a perfect section to find something fascinating.

I found it, all right.

I was browsing through a couple of historic photograph books, which I found mildly amusing, when suddenly a word caught my eye: *Nudes.* There it was just right out in the open, staring at me and calling my name. It was the title of a book that featured black-and-white images of naked women.

I felt forbidden excitement just reading the title. I told myself I shouldn't be so interested, but with hormones surging through my body I just couldn't take my eyes away.

I looked around to see if anyone in my family was near. The coast was clear. I slowly reached for the book, opened its cover carefully, and for the next five minutes stared wide-eyed at the enthralling pages. The book was intended as art, but I knew that art wasn't on my mind. Somehow I instinctively knew I was diminishing the worth of the women in the images by the way I was looking at them. I knew our family held a value for honoring other people, and I was pretty sure I wasn't looking at those people to honor them. But I couldn't look away.

Suddenly I heard a family member yell that it was time to go. I quickly closed the book and shoved it under the others I had been holding. I looked around carefully, replaced the books on the shelf, and followed my siblings out of the store. But as I stepped into the cool Colorado night, I felt the guilt wash over me.

I looked at my family walking, smiling, and laughing, and suddenly I felt dirty in their presence. I thought about how "good" each of them was and how "bad" they would think I was if they only knew what I had done. For the next few hours, as we headed home and got ready for bed, I couldn't shake the overwhelming and obsessive feeling of filth covering me.

I guess to most this seems like a pretty normal occurrence and something too small to be affected deeply about, especially in the oversexualized culture we live in.

But for me as a young teen with a desire to be a Superman, to live purely, to do the right thing—and yes, as a teen with

OCD and anxiety disorder—the failure felt so visceral, so permanent. It stood out in my mind as a dark blemish on my soul. It reared its ugly head in the face of everything I wanted to be, allowing my obsessive mind to latch on and push me to the brink.

Maybe this is the way every first sexual violation should feel to young men who seek to be pure and are thrust into a world of compromise. (Guilt can be useful when it is for the right reason.) On the other hand, I wouldn't wish this torment on anyone. It was excruciating.

By the time I was in bed, the guilt was eating me alive, to the point where I was certain I would feel no peace that night. Incessant feelings of shame covered my mind, and no matter how hard I tried to push them out or wish them away, they came barging back in.

I sat up, hot with sweat and frustration. The freezing night air hit me with a shock as I threw off the covers. I looked out my window—in this house, it was on the second floor—at the snow-covered plains that drifted into the nearby foothills, and I took a breath in to calm myself. A breath out. Another one in—but to no avail. The accusing voices still insisted on making themselves known.

I briefly wondered what it would be like to dive out that window and silence the voices for good. No more guilt, no more shame, no more uncontrollable thoughts slamming into my consciousness with no consideration for my well-being. I thought about the stories I had heard in youth group about those who had taken their lives for various reasons.

And for the first time I understood why people might resort to that end. Maybe they were desperate to silence the voices of doubt, shame, fear, and hopelessness.

I thought about my family, sleeping peacefully just beyond my closed door and down the hall. Even though they were near, I felt a huge separation between us, sequestering me to battle my thoughts alone.

We have all made mistakes both big and small. Even those who aren't teenagers with OCD know what it's like when the guilt and shame of our darker actions separate us from those we love. Most of us know what it's like to live with inner voices that tell us we have messed up or are not good enough. And it's all too easy to allow those voices to affect the way we see the world and how we relate to the people around us.

The amazing thing about having a loving Creator who freely offers grace, forgiveness, and redemption is that no matter how loud the voices of darkness scream, the Voice of light will always be louder.

But not if we don't choose it.

Yes, who we listen to is a choice—maybe not always a conscious one, but a choice all the same. It's a choice that makes all the difference to our lives and our relationships, including our relationship with God—because it eventually determines who we become.

When we choose to listen to God, He grants us freedom from what we've done and who we've been. When we heed the voice of our Creator telling us we are redeemed, sufficient, and made new, we no longer have to be bound by guilt and shame that separate us from who and what we love.

Sally

As Nathan started foraying out into the world of teenagers, his hormones took him on a wild and woolly path.

That's actually true of most teenagers—it certainly was for mine. I think most of my children turned a corner toward becoming more mature adults at around twenty to twenty-three, but the years before that provided constant challenges, different for each child. Whatever is a smaller issue during elementary years seems to become magnified in the teen years—louder, stronger, worse, more!

All children long to fit in, to be liked, to appear normal during a movement from childhood to adulthood. Pushing against expectations, ideals, and authority is normal behavior, and it accelerates during the teen years. And for outside-the-box kids, who long to be like everyone else, this tendency can be magnified. The result can be a very bumpy road through adolescence.

Nathan made a lot of foolish mistakes as a teen, in other words—multiple parking tickets, losing his driver's license and keys, getting in trouble in more small ways than I have pages to write. There were times when I wondered if anything we had ever taught him or any of our training had made a difference.

I know I will never know the extent of his bad choices. I am quite sure he has never "told all." Suffice it to say that his teen years were very challenging for us and probably for him.

Yet Nathan also continued to grow and stretch in ways that gave us hope. He practiced making wise decisions, little by little, among all of those foolish ones—and he appeared to learn from his mistakes. He seemed to resist drinking and moral compromises even when kids in his church group were compromising in many ways. And he drew us in as confidants for himself and his friends. We were the trusted parents who would sit with his buddies late into the night.

All the kids his age seemed to love Nathan. He was a pied piper of sorts because he was so much fun. But he also began to emerge, surprisingly, as a confident communicator in front of crowds.

Because he had played drums for years to get out his energy before we read, he was invited to be in a band by a couple of friends he had met at church. (This was the season of life when I began to use earplugs.) Eventually, in a concert played in front of hundreds of his peers, he was the entertaining emcee for the evening.

"Mom," he often told me, "I want to be a light." He deliberately pursued shining that light into the darkness of many lost friends—and he had a lot of them. He always seemed to have a heart for the confused, rebellious ones. His choice of some very foolish companions led to many confrontations and arguments, but it also evidenced his loving heart.

Because we wanted to teach our kids hospitality—and because we preferred to have Nathan's friends where we could see them—we encouraged him to bring any- and everybody into our home. Hungry for direction and affirmation and in need of light, redemption, and restoration, many flocked to our home because of him. Making our home a haven for every teen—crazy, lost, shy, loud, and without direction or love—was important to Nathan.

I made literally thousands of cookies, brownies, and pizzas during these years because I always wanted Nathan to want to come home, to want to bring his friends here. Some of our guests dubbed me Dude Mama. Once I even brought some boys in for cooking lessons so they could invite their girlfriends to our home for a "fancy" dinner.

I made a deliberate choice to put aside many of my own needs and time commitments during this time in order to involve all our kids deeply in this ministry of hospitality. Doing this meant that our children and their friends perceived God as one who welcomes all. It also gave some of those teens a much-needed safe place to hang out.

It is possible that Nathan's differences actually protected him from a lot of temptation during these years. For instance, drugs and dealers were all around Nathan during those years, but he tells us he was never tempted to use. And when he did do something wrong, he would usually confess it immediately to Clay and me just to get the obsessive thought out of his head. He did this the morning after the incident with the *Nudes* book at the bookstore.

It seems that everywhere our children turn these days, they encounter forces that battle for their minds, souls, consciences, and convictions. And we as parents are responsible to fight on their side, to do everything we can to give them the advantage.

For a young hormonal teen who wants to do the right thing, for instance, living in our culture can be deeply frustrating. Sexual images are everywhere—from "tasteful" nudes in an art book to suggestive ads to Internet porn—and they're absurdly easy to access.

The art book at Borders was Nathan's first exposure to nude images, but both our sons encountered them a little later on a photography website. We had given them cameras so they could learn how to take artistic photos to display online. Unfortunately, their love for photography, which we had given to them, led them to less-than-wholesome images.

Yet both boys came to us to confess what they had found. Understanding that we would forgive them, help them, and stand beside them no matter what they had done laid a foundation of trust that served us throughout the teen years and on into adulthood. (In addition, Clay set guardian eyes on the computers of both boys, made a pact of accountability with them, and stayed in touch about these matters so that they had a champion on their side to help them pursue a life of integrity.)

When children understand that their parents accept them whether they are behaviorally perfect or not, that they can trust the grown-ups with anything, then they will be more likely to seek their parents' help when they have engaged in more serious misbehavior.

All of us fail in many ways, parents and children alike— and this dynamic can be exaggerated during the high-pressure teenage years. (It certainly was for Nathan and me.) During this time, God's gift of His Holy Spirit can be especially helpful, leading us in the ways we should go, convicting us of sin, and bringing us God's comfort. So can the words of Scripture, especially when it has been put to memory. I have always said that God's Word is His vocabulary. The Spirit of God can speak to teens through memorized verses when they are away from our homes and our influence.

Speaking of the Spirit, I believe parents are to play a similar role in the lives of our children. No, we're not called to play God in their lives! But we are there to encourage, to confront, to remind, to teach the ways of God so that our kids can find health and peace in their paths of life. We don't usually force or control, but we do nudge and influence. And we retain our role as helpers whenever we can.

Parents are also called to model God for our teens. If we are gentle, loving, kind, forgiving, then our children will have a picture from us that God is also gracious, kind, loving, forgiving. Jesus told Peter that He had prayed for him when Peter turned his back on Him. In the same way, we can show His heart to our kids by giving them grace but also calling them back to their foundations.

Passing on an understanding of biblical values, holding up and teaching righteous principles for living, coaching our children in making wise decisions amidst confusing voices—all these are essential to helping teens mature and develop a strong faith. And so is allowing our children to fail. Just as a toddler falls when learning to walk, so our children will fall from time to time on the way toward adulthood.

I know from experience how easy it is to become discouraged when we fail as parents or when our children fail (or refuse) to live up to what we expect of them. But failure is not a reason to give up! It is a reason to regroup, refresh our vision, and then continue moving forward.

Righteousness is a journey of moving from immaturity toward maturity. If we want our children to continue on this journey, we owe it to them to be sound companions. We must demonstrate that they can trust us with their failures.

This is doubly true, I believe, for our outside-the-box children. Though they may present an extra challenge during the teen years, they need our support, our practical help, and our belief in their future more than ever. Learning the ropes of adult responsibility and the consequences of their choices must be a part of the progress they make before they leave our homes.

"Differents" long for affirmation, love, and affection even more than ever during the teen years, even if their behavior is somewhat erratic. Understanding and liking who they are and providing those life-giving words of encouragement are essential to their eventually becoming self-actualized.

Parents of different and usually immature teens are often tempted to tighten the controls and try harder to prevent the kids from making mistakes. I know I felt that temptation with Nathan. I sometimes wondered whether he would ever be able to get a job or live away from home.

But Clay and I believed that if Nathan was ever going to be somewhat independent, we had to let him start practicing while he was still at home. So we gave him freedom even when we weren't sure what the outcome would be.

Yes, we were there to walk him through the foolish decisions and inevitable mistakes rising from immaturity. But we also tried our best to let go and let Nathan make his own choices, especially when he showed his growing maturity.

As Nathan progressed through his teen years, his conversations with me showed more and more engagement in wanting to be a man of God. His desire to become God's man flamed higher, fanned by our words of affirmation and our trust that God would lead him, our belief that he would act wisely by the standards held fast in our family. We learned that trust and freedom at the right time is a strong motivator for kids to live into their parents' informed expectations.

We must remember always that it is God's responsibility to lead our children, even our different children. We are called to love them and guide them to the best of our ability, to teach them that their choices have consequences, and to provide a strong foundation for stewarding their lives. But we are not ultimately responsible for all that happens to them.

We must remember that God loves our teens—and our outside-the-box teens—even more than we do. We are merely a tool in His hands for raising them, a conduit for His faithful love through all the seasons of their lives.

CHAPTER 11

Naming the Enemy

....

Why Acceptance Is Only a First Step

NATHAN

"It's my belief that you have obsessive-compulsive disorder and attention-deficit/hyperactivity disorder, plus a couple of processing learning disorders."

The words fell out of the specialist's mouth and seemed to echo in the small office.

The specialist and my mom looked at me, awaiting my response. But I didn't really have one at the moment. I didn't exactly know what to think. So I turned my head and gazed out the window, trying to process what this all meant.

For as long as I could remember, I could tell my mind

worked differently from those of other people, and I had experienced a lot of confusion, anger, and pain because of it. But up until now, all my quirks and behavioral differences had been a mystery, seemingly striking at will like a nameless assailant.

But now, in this little whitewashed office, in the middle of a Wednesday afternoon, my demons had been named. Or lettered—because most of these seemed to be summed up with letters: OCD. ADHD. ODD.

I had apparently had these letters all my fifteen years, but this was the first time they had been officially used to explain my differences. And I didn't dispute that the letters applied to me. I was the only person I knew who either couldn't stay focused on one thing at a time or had a fear of touching doorknobs. Recently I had been taking five showers a day and washing my hands until they bled, so I accepted the diagnosis that I had the *OC* (obsessive compulsions). But there was something about the *D* (disorder) I didn't like. It made me feel as if my personality and mind needed to be fixed—when I had been brought up to believe that I was especially designed by God.

So did God make a mistake? Was my mind a mistake?

But while I wrestled with the new title, at the same time I found an odd comfort in the letters. In a funny way it was a relief knowing that I wasn't just crazy. Or if I was, at least there were other people out there that the letters applied to, so I wasn't both crazy and alone. If my mind was a disorder, at least I wasn't the only one. (It's funny how much difference simply knowing you're not alone in something can make.)

WE MUST LEARN TO DESIRE THE LIGHT
GOD OFFERS MORE THAN THE SAFETY
AND COMFORT OF THE DARKNESS
WHERE WE ALREADY LIVE.

I felt something else in that moment too. After years of battling symptoms that baffled me as much as they baffled others, I felt relief.

My enemy was no longer invisible. And now that I could see what I was up against, I could begin the fight. By acknowledging the broken places in my mind and heart, I could begin the process of being put back together—and becoming the man I was meant to be.

....

"You're perfect the way you are."

"Just accept yourself, and you'll be happy."

"Don't ever change."

I have heard platitudes like these all my life. And I confess I became so accustomed to hearing them that I didn't realize the damage they can do if we actually believe them.

As with every effective lie, there is a hint of beautiful truth in each one of these. There's truth in the fact that we don't need to live by others' standards and that there are things that we simply are not, cannot, and should not strive to be. And yes, accepting and loving ourselves is an imperative for a healthy life.

But does it stop there?

If we take statements like these as saying there is no higher standard for us to live up to, no versions of ourselves we should strive for beyond the one we currently inhabit, I think we do our hearts, souls, bodies, and relationships a grand disservice.

We were not made to "never change."

We were not redeemed by God simply to "accept ourselves as we are"—and stay there—at any point in time.

We were never created to find happiness in the status quo or to fool ourselves into thinking that our broken, imperfect lives are just the way they are supposed to be.

I believe in God. I believe in a design behind the universe. I believe in purpose. When you look at any facet of life, you will find the fingerprints of an Artist who weaves together both the physical and abstract into a beautiful intention to live into. God tells us we are "fearfully and wonderfully made." And the essence of Jesus' message urges us to realize that we were put into a story that moves us forward into greater beauty and fullness as we continue to follow it.

But there is another factor at play—our own darkness, selfishness, rebellion, and reluctance to work or feel pain. It's our desire to do things our way, apart from God's design and apart from His call to live into the person we were created to be. This is the definition of *broken* for all of us born into this fallen world.

There was a time right after high school when I was trying to find my path in life, to discover who I was supposed to be and where I was supposed to go, but things weren't going well. With few tangible results or sure answers, my anxiety spiked (the OCD didn't help) and depression worked its way over me, leading me to cope in unhealthy ways.

At one point, tired of the worry and the disappointment of being unhealthy, depressed, and forty pounds overweight,

I gave up. At the time, I actually believed that giving up was a good thing. I said to myself, "This is who I am, and I accept myself."

But that wasn't exactly true. I wasn't really accepting myself. I was just denying myself the opportunity to be the better person I could become.

Deep down, I was very unhappy with who I was at the moment. But facing that reality was painful and something I wasn't willing to do. When I stared at the realization that becoming a person of health took time, healthy eating, exercise, pain, and patience, I decided it was a journey I didn't want to take. And so I justified my unhealthy behavior and anesthetized the pain I felt with escapes and distractions that made me feel better temporarily but hurt me more in the long run. My so-called self-acceptance was mostly just a justification to remain in my own darkness.

To simply accept ourselves the way we are denies ourselves the beauty of becoming who we could be. This truth finds its way into every facet of life—physical, mental, professional, and so on. So often, when we are faced with shortcomings or struggles in our lives, our first reaction is to deny, justify, escape, or anesthetize instead of facing our inevitable brokenness head on and making the harder and more time-consuming choice to be an agent of life in the world that so needs it.

The hard truth is that we live in an imperfect world, one that is filled with sickness, disease, abuse, pain, addiction, injustice, and fear. And every one of us has been touched in one way or another by the brokenness of this fallen world. Every one of us has baggage. Not one of us is perfect, whole, or complete—"no, not one" (Romans 3:10, NKJV). None of us even comes close.

But the beauty, as I see it, is that although our loving Creator accepts us just as we are, in the middle of our brokenness and pain, He doesn't stop there. Instead, He offers us what no one else can—a story that can lead us forward. But to live into that story, we must stop accepting our brokenness as "just the way we are" and stop telling ourselves and the world that such acceptance is healthy. We must stop looking to escape the hurt and instead learn to recognize and face our pain and brokenness.

We must learn to desire the light He offers more than the safety and comfort of the darkness where we already live.

In a culture that seeks only to anesthetize, escape, and ignore hurt, I believe we are called to experience, acknowledge, and *feel* the pain of life so that redemption can be achieved. Because only when we have walked through the dark can we appreciate and crave the light. Pain can be the muscle that tears to make us stronger and the surgery that cuts to make us whole. So instead of running from the hurt, we must instead embrace it, own it, live with it, and trust in God's ability to use what feels like death as the catalyst for finding life.

Those whose goal is to "feel better about themselves" often find their journey one of escape, addiction, blame, denial— a cycle of deeper pain. But those who are actually dedicated to becoming their better selves will have a story of hard work, realization, dedication, introspection, and humility—which will lead ultimately toward strength and wholeness.

Sally

Clouds of discouragement rained inside our car as I drove on the crowded freeway. Fifteen-year-old Nathan and I were on the way to visit yet another counselor. I tried to speak positively about all the great things I had heard about the woman we were about to meet. But to tell the truth, neither of us felt very hopeful. Over the past two years we had visited three different counselors, looking for someone to help us define some of the issues and give us some idea how to move forward.

So far, nobody we had consulted had worked out. Instead we had gotten pat answers, accusations of bad parenting, even diagnoses of demon possession. And we had no confidence that this new counselor would be able to help. But we felt we needed to try.

Entering the simply decorated waiting room, Nathan plopped on a seat as far away from me as he could while I filled out one more set of forms to describe why we were there and what his particular issues were.

A young, hip woman greeted us pleasantly. "Looking forward to getting to know you both. Come into my office."

I managed a whisper-prayer as we followed her through the door. "Please, Lord. Please let this one actually help us."

After administering a thirty-minute test, the counselor announced, "Nathan, you fit the exact marks for obsessive-compulsive disorder. And according to this test, you are one of the most OCD kids I have seen in my practice. I think I can give you some answers—what to be aware of, how to find help. And you know what, Nathan? Most clinically diagnosed OCD kids are very artistic and often very bright. I bet you are one of those!"

I could tell from Nathan's face that these were words of life—a deep salve to his soul. At last someone outside our family seemed to understand what we were going through. At last someone cared enough to suggest that Nathan might actually have some good attributes—and a future.

There would be many bumps and falls as Nathan moved through his teen years, but he also made steady forward progress. And this was due in part to his diagnosis by that specialist and several others.

Finally his differences had names.

Finally we understood that we were dealing with mental illness that could be clinically verified and treated.

Finally we had dependable support in addressing his issues.

We then made a commitment to Nathan: "Let's pray about this and consider what are the best ways you can treat your symptoms, improve your skills, embody your vision for life, and become the best man you can be. Then we will help you and support you any way we can."

Our vision with Nathan and for him was that God had

created him to flourish, to grow, to become strong enough to fulfill his God-given destiny.

What we had to do was figure out—together—how that would happen.

....

In his preteen and early teen years, Nathan began to exhibit many extreme issues in regard to his OCD—behavior that indicated true emotional anxiety and mental illness. He had shown obsessive tendencies as a little boy, but we had been able to work with him in most of those areas. However, when hormones hit, the OCD escalated to levels that helped us understand he was struggling with more than a personality preference.

Clearly Nathan needed help—more help than we could give him. After seeking the advice of friends and physicians, I took Nathan and another child to different counselors to have them assessed.

What I learned in that process is that not all physicians and not all counselors are equally helpful.

One told us that our child suffered from "generational sin, probably caused by pornography in a previous generation," another that our children harbored demons that needed to be cast out. This type of counsel was very disturbing to my adolescent children and was not helpful at all. They needed medical evaluation, not mysterious guessing at what was at the root of their problem.

Yet another counselor from a reputable, well-known

organization told Nathan, behind closed doors, that he was mentally ill because his parents were self-centered from being in ministry—in other words, that *we* were his problem. Since Nathan had always had a strong and healthy relationship with us, this advice was strange and discouraging to him. He actually came home from the appointment saying, "Why did you waste my time on this crazy man? He didn't even know you or me or interview you. He just went to your website and deduced that you must be my problem because of all the books you've written."

During this time, we took him to our general practitioner physician, who prescribed a very mild depression medication that also helps some OCD patients. When Nathan experienced some improvement, we realized that the right kind of medications, especially the ones specifically targeting OCD, might help control his symptoms more effectively.

Finally, we sought out a counseling office that actually did testing for OCD and gave specific counseling for adolescents with this diagnosis. This counselor was amazingly helpful. She encouraged Nathan greatly and made him feel good about himself, while teaching him some principles of cognitive therapy and some techniques to help him control his symptoms. She made us realize that professional therapists who have studied specific psychological issues can be very helpful in providing positive instruction and therapy.

As Nathan grew into adulthood, it was recommended that he find a psychiatrist who specialized in OCD. This psychiatrist's evaluations also made Nathan feel understood, accepted, and less isolated. Instead of being labeled as a behavioral problem, Nathan could receive treatment for a medical issue he had been born with. This doctor prescribed a relatively new medication that has few side effects and great results. The progress with his new medication was marked. We saw big changes in Nathan's basic contentment and less agitation with life.

We found that professionally trained counselors who had appropriate clinical education made all the difference in helping us understand Nathan's differences and giving us tools to handle those differences. These skilled consultants provided us with useful insight and actively promoted Nathan's healing and forward progress. They also helped us feel less alone and isolated by assuring us that Nathan wasn't the only one to struggle with his particular disabilities. And they made it possible for Nathan to receive medication that helped with some of his most extreme symptoms.

....

"Getting help" for different children can be a fraught decision, especially for Christian families. Everyone seems to have an opinion—or a judgment—about what is appropriate and what is not appropriate, and the multitude of voices can be confusing. I don't want to add to that noise, especially for struggling families. So I'll just add a few observations based on our experience and leave it at that.

First of all, by all means do seek help! Look for all the help you can get. And when one approach doesn't prove helpful or just doesn't feel right, try another one. Keep asking and seeking and knocking until you find what you need.

Second, finding the best source of help for your situation will require self-education and research, close observation, careful discernment, plus lots and lots of prayer. Every human being is a mysterious creation, and both parent and child need wisdom from God to know how to move forward.

Third, remember that you are the expert on your child and his or her most important advocate. Even if you don't completely understand your child's differences—I certainly didn't!—you still know more about him or her than anyone else. Don't be afraid to say no to what doesn't seem to fit your situation or to say yes to an approach your family or friends may disapprove of. (And don't assume that a person who claims to be a counselor automatically has a handle on the issue.) As the parent, you can ask God for wisdom and then use your own knowledge and experience to evaluate what you think is best for your child.

Fourth, don't expect easy answers or a miracle fix. Life rarely works that way.

But fifth, don't underestimate what your child—and God—can do. I have seen many different children move well beyond their disabilities to accomplish far more than what their counselors, physicians, teachers, or the parents themselves would have predicted.

And finally, don't try to use our family's experience as an exact template for your family. Every child is unique and requires a unique approach. At the same time, I hope that hearing our story brings you some encouragement—because there really is hope!

....

I've written a lot in this book about the importance of accepting our different children just as they are, providing a place for them to be themselves, and appreciating God's design for them. This is absolutely crucial—but it needs to be balanced with doing our best to help our children grow and move forward in their lives.

Parents who feel deep sympathy or compassion for their children's issues can easily become enablers for their children and actually limit their progress. A parent who becomes paralyzed with a diagnosis or limits his or her child to a particular prognosis could be harming the child.

This story of being parents to these children is a process of doing the most we can to help our children in a practical way, considering their various issues, doing our very best to support their dreams, and then trusting God to fill in beyond our human capacities.

Our parenting plan for raising Nathan involved giving him a vision for growing strong inside and exercising his mental and moral muscle. It included training his character as far as it would go as well as supporting him in practical ways and putting him in situations where he could reasonably succeed.

But Nathan surprised us by doing so much more than we expected in these areas. He developed some amazing strengths and skills and even acquired some jobs we had never considered for him—such as acting in national commercials and getting bit parts in television. Consequently, we began to pay attention to what he wanted, not just what we thought he should logically pursue. And we prayed with him that God would open doors for him to do what he wanted to do in life.

Nathan stayed unflinchingly strong in his confidence that this would happen. "God will do it in His time, Mom." But to be honest, I had my doubts.

Nathan's dreams were so big, so expansive. He wanted to be an actor, a screenwriter, to make Hollywood films that reflected the Christian worldview. And his differences could be so daunting. I had trouble imagining his prayers being answered in the way he expected.

But Nathan was my son. So I prayed for his dreams because he wanted us to. I prayed because *he* kept on praying.

As the years went by, I would be reminded again and again that the Lord hears not just my prayers, but also the fervent prayers and hopes of my children.

Nathan prayed his heart out, asking God to make it possible for him to pursue his dreams. "Mom, there needs to be light in the entertainment industry. I have been asking God every day to open doors for me there. But I'm trying to keep leaning on Him and trusting in His power."

Nathan also said, "Mama, it would be terrible for an athlete to practice his whole life and never have the opportunity to compete. Trust me, Mama, and let's trust God together. I think God is answering my prayers."

As I continued to pray for Nathan's dreams and his future, I found myself thinking about Daniel from the Bible. Daniel was a godly man who lived amidst one of the most wicked and immoral cultures in all of history. But he stayed strong and influenced thousands of people for God's Kingdom.

So I began praying more specifically: "God, be with our own Daniel as he enters his Babylon." I prayed (and still pray) every day that Nathan would make Daniel choices.

Eventually this stepping out in faith led Nathan to train as an actor, to write his first screenplay and his first self-produced movie, to develop a production company, and to author three books. It led him first to New York, then to Los Angeles, and then back to New York. It led him to hustling for parts, scouring the Internet for auditions and showing up faithfully for any job he could find. (He never got one gig through his agent.)

Even after Nathan left home, I kept up with him almost daily to help him with anything he needed and to call him to accountability to live a life of character. But a very big step for me was to trust that even though he continued to carry all of his issues wherever he went, God still had a place where he could exercise his strengths and faith and be able to learn to flourish.

Faith with outside-the-box kids means trusting them to do beyond what we can imagine and trusting God to keep them in His care. That's what we had to do with our son.

And let me stress once more that this story is unique to Nathan. I would never encourage anyone else to send their young adult to Hollywood or New York City unless they had prayed long and hard and made provisions to help hold them accountable. But I do think God desires us to trust Him and encourage our children to pursue their potential as far as it takes them—providing training, instruction, and vision but also being willing to stretch beyond current limitations.

Nathan confirmed this when he called me one day from New York, where he was taking acting classes, "Mama, this is the first place I have ever felt like I fit in. Everyone in my classes is outside-the-box creative and loves to pretend great stories. We all understand one another.

"This is definitely the place I need to be!"

....

Many of you who have read my blog or books know, since then, that Nathan has written a book about his time in New York City, where God met him amidst all the glitz and glitter. *Wisdom Chasers*[7] is filled with personal stories of his journey of faith as an aspiring filmmaker in the Big Apple.

The years have matured him, taught him to become a warrior in a place of many spiritual and moral challenges, and given him the discipline and endurance to pursue the dreams God put on his heart. As his mom, I regularly sought God in his behalf and prayed for him so very often. I had a choice to make—to believe in his dreams and to support this seemingly impossible pursuit or to tell him that his dreams were foolish and that he would always be limited in what he could do.

But I believe all of us need to feel that ultimately our lives matter and that the desires of our hearts are placed there by God in order to lead us to the Kingdom work He would have us fulfill. Besides, our home was founded on the idea that God uses ordinary people who are filled with His Spirit to bring His Kingdom into all realms of the world. If this was true for the more "normal" members of our family, I had to believe it was also true for Nathan.

And so we have become advocates for Nathan—both before the throne of heaven and in daily life through phone calls, e-mails, visits, and spoken words of affirmation and correction. You will still find me on the phone with Nathan every day as a cheerleader. His life has required me to be one who pursues, gives time, listens, talks, and gives support for hours at a time. But the sacrifice of time this requires must be understood in the context of the many sacrifices we as parents are called on to make through the years.

I'm convinced that as Nathan walks with God and follows hard after Him, God will use this talented young man in ways far beyond what I could have imagined for him. But his faith does not come from a vacuum, but from a mentoring, growing relationship with parents who invested themselves so that he and his siblings might have foundations of faith to draw from.

Nathan had some detours through the years of his young adult life. No small book can contain all of the stories of the ups and downs. Yet I am grateful that Nathan was able to get back on course when he felt he had failed, seeking to become strong, gradually learning to work harder, and pursuing his God on a journey of faith through the usual valleys and storms of young adulthood and the particular challenges posed by his differences. But it was understanding his part in becoming strong that gave him the vision to keep going, to pick himself up one more time, and to trust God to open the right doors as he worked hard toward his dreams.

BY ACKNOWLEDGING THE BROKEN
PLACES IN MY MIND AND HEART, I COULD
BEGIN THE PROCESS OF BEING PUT BACK
TOGETHER—AND BECOMING THE MAN
I WAS MEANT TO BE.

CHAPTER 12

Beyond "Why Me?"

....

Facing the Reality of "Always Different"

NATHAN

The blood was rising to my face, and I felt my head becoming familiarly warm as it sank into my hands. I sat hunched over on the stairs outside my basement room, next to the bathroom, too afraid to move, not knowing what to do.

Just a few minutes ago everything had been all right. I was packing my bags, ready to leave home and head back to California to continue pursuing my dreams of becoming an actor. Back in Los Angeles I had been making new friends and had even met a cute girl I was excited to see at church again.

But now, in the matter of a few tragic minutes, my whole world had gone dark.

Had someone died? Had there been an intruder? An accident?

No, nothing like that.

The event that had sent me spiraling into chaos was an old toilet that had backed up and spilled out onto the bathroom floor.

To most this would be a minor inconvenience that a couple of towels and a wrench could fix. But to my twenty-two-year-old mind on OCD it held more weight than anyone could see. In my mind it meant that everything on this floor of the house was dirty. My clothes, the Christmas gifts I was taking home to Los Angeles, my personal belongings—all were contaminated beyond redemption.

Logically I knew that this wasn't true, but logic is no match for an anxiety attack. I also knew that in just a couple of minutes I would need to leave the house with my luggage to catch my plane back to California. But the weight of my contaminated thoughts kept me frozen on the stairs.

This is so silly, I told myself. *Nothing's dirty. Just get up like a normal person, grab your bags, and hug your family good-bye.* But the thought of touching the people I loved and possibly contaminating them, too, put knots in my stomach.

I felt tears push their way out of the corners of my eyes. I quickly brushed them away, ashamed of myself.

What would all of my new friends think of me, a twenty-two-year-old man crying over a little water? What would the new girl I liked think of me if she could see what a pathetic sight I was right then?

As I thought of where I was and what I was doing, for the first time in a long time I hated myself.

I hated the fact that I was different.

I hated the fact that I, a six-foot-three, two-hundred-pound grown man, had been brought to tears by an overflowing toilet.

I let out a silent scream as I raked my fingers through my hair. Another tear hit the ground, and I looked up at the whitewashed ceiling.

"How could You do this to me?" I whispered aloud to God. "How could You let my mind be so messed up? Why can't I just be normal?" I slammed my fist into the ground, and a powerful sob burst forth from a deeply imbedded place in my soul.

To this day I still have moments of profound pain when I feel the harsh separation between me and the rest of the world. I can see the stark differences between me and normal. And as much as I would like to have overcome it, I find myself still struggling with the same battles I've always had.

I think I've always held on to the hope that someday all my differences would just disappear, that eventually I would no longer have any battles to fight, that someday I would finally win. But then, year after year, I would find myself back at the same place, slamming my fist into the ground, looking up to God and crying, "Why me?"

But here's the interesting thing about all those years of

crying to and at God. I never really got an explanation. But somehow, each and every time I asked the question, I found myself closer to Him than the time before. This allowed me to slowly make progress in the battles I continue to fight.

I think no matter who we are or what we believe, we all have times when we look up at the invisible God and cry out, "Why?" or "How could You do this?" Maybe you've been like me, wrestling with a crippling anxiety attack that just won't release its grip. Or perhaps it's something else. But all of us have times when we don't understand what is happening to us and life feels like too much to handle. Times when "Why?" seems like the only honest and rational response.

And maybe, just maybe, that's not a bad thing.

The truth is, we live in a deeply fractured world, and we don't always have a choice about being broken. But we do have a choice about where we let our brokenness lead us.

We can follow it into escape or addiction.

But we can also follow it straight to God. To the One who knows us inside and out—with all our mistakes, broken parts, insecurities, and battles—and who still loves us.

To the One who can not only handle our anger and our frustration and our questions, but can use them to transform us.

As we practice running back to our Creator in times of trial, we find ourselves in the place where healing begins.

Sally

Relief washed over me as I waved good-bye to Sarah and Joel, who were heading on a post-Christmas road trip to Boston. Joy was packing to return to her classes. And Nathan would be flying back to Los Angeles in just a few short hours.

I couldn't wait.

Having all our grown kids here for the holidays was always a joy—but it could feel like a burden, too. Home was now a refuge from the world of adult responsibilities for them. They longed for homemade meals, sleep, fun, and total relaxation. And I was the one who was supposed to make all this happen—in the midst of my already packed schedule.

I'm not saying that having them all home wasn't worth the trouble. It was! My children are truly my best friends, and I love having them together, re-creating the traditions we have cherished through the years. But I also love the quiet that comes when they head back to the lives they have built elsewhere.

I hated to admit that I was especially glad for Nathan to leave, at least for a little while. But being told what we could and couldn't eat and being asked to wash our hands when we touched certain things becomes trying after about the third day. The petty arguments and the sense that we were walking on eggshells gave an underlying tension to our days. I was weary and ready for a break.

Having three children who had OCD, two of them severe, always created an extra level of stress in our household.

Trying to understand, always getting something wrong, and being corrected daily made for challenging days. But even worse was the fact that other members of the family, including Clay, didn't always "get" our children's issues.

I had done a fair amount of research since Nathan's diagnosis and had come to understand his brain issues a little better. (I highly recommend Bruce Hyman and Cherry Pedrick's *The OCD Workbook*.[8]) But Clay tended to think that if the kids just tried harder they could overcome their "attitudes." And whenever the OCD, the ADHD, and the personality disorders reared their heads, he tended to go into retreat.

This issue had already come up during this holiday visit. After dinner one night, Clay stood up and headed in the direction of Nathan's computer to help him download a program they had been discussing. From experience, I knew that Nathan would not touch the computer anymore if Clay had touched it without washing his hands first. Jumping up to stand between them, I pronounced too loudly, "Please don't touch it. Please don't help him tonight. Your hands are dirty."

"My hands are not dirty. I have just been eating dinner with a fork."

Understandably, Clay was offended and frustrated with both my sudden action and Nathan's seeming unreasonableness.

But I was the one who had been to all the counselors with Nathan. I was the one who had read the books about OCD. I was the "confessor" who had listened to all of my OCD kids' deepest guilt thoughts, and so I understood the issues a little bit more.

More to the point, I simply did not want to face one more incident before Nathan left. I wanted to put the Christmas holidays to rest with as much peace as possible.

It didn't work. Clay retreated under a dark cloud, trying to understand, wanting to help Nathan but being rebuffed. And the tension went on.

I want to stress that Clay loves Nathan. He's a devoted father to him and all our kids. And in the years that followed this incident, he has come to understand OCD better. But it still takes both of us trying to respond appropriately to Nathan's issues, which can be unpredictable. It's still hard to avoid doing something that sets him off and sends him spiraling downward into a hole, though these days, after years of treatment, Nathan struggles less and is so much more patient and consistently loving. Finding a good psychiatrist and the right medication to suit his issues has brought great relief to him and to us as well.

Back then, however, when we were just starting to figure it all out, dealing with Nathan's differences was harder—yet another reason I was glad when the time for Nathan's departure drew near. He would fly back to the safe, secure, controlled environment of his California apartment, and Clay and I could stop walking on eggshells.

But I was in for yet another surprise.

Glancing at my watch, I realized it was almost time for Nathan to be picked up for his ride to the airport. Where was he? I ran down the stairs toward his basement room to find out.

I found him on the bottom step, still in the wrinkled T-shirt and gray sport shorts he wore as pajamas, arms hugging his knees as tightly as possible. Head low, tears dripping, he swayed back and forth. Gloom hovered like a cloud around his whole being.

Dread squeezed my heart and familiar knots formed in my stomach as I searched the file drawers of my mind to make sense of what I was seeing. Imagining that something terrible had rocked his world, I slid to sit silently beside him.

"I can't go to the airport," he said in a voice full of despair. "I don't have any clothes that I can wear."

Searching in the recesses of my mind for what he could possibly mean, I gently reminded him that he had just received some brand-new clothes for Christmas.

"But Mom, you don't understand. When the toilet overflowed this morning, it contaminated everything in the basement, including all my clothes. If I wear them, I'll be dirty. I'm *already* dirty because I was sleeping down here in my bedroom when it happened."

Just in my eyesight were Nathan's new clothes, pristine, still in the package, clean as could be. His room was far from the bathroom in question, but just the fact that it was on the same floor meant that everything in it was contaminated in his eyes.

My mind raced, flooded at first with practical concerns. *What can we do? The car will be here any second. Nathan's plane won't wait for him. The ticket is nonrefundable.*

Then a flood of sympathy washed those thoughts away. Once again, the depths of anguish and struggle Nathan faced every day, just living a normal life, broke my heart, and my own helplessness haunted me.

I could not fix Nathan's pain.

I could not remove his humiliation or soothe his fears.

I could not convince him that his thoughts were completely irrational and unfounded.

I could not find relief for my mama-heart anguish.

Once more, my mother love could not remove what God had allowed. Nathan, so idealistic, so full of insight into people and issues, so articulate, so loving—and yet so burdened by his issues—had to carry the paralyzing fear and darkness alone.

I wanted to wrap him in my arms to comfort him, but I resisted. This was another sacrifice I had been forced to make in the years since his OCD got worse. I could not comfort my son through a motherly embrace or kiss his cheek in affection the way I did with my other children. Being touched made him feel contaminated, even when the touch came from someone he loved. At this moment, though, he was more worried about contaminating me, his beloved mama. He had been in the basement when the toilet overflowed. To his mind, touching me would make me as dirty as he was.

After almost a half hour of praying, talking, reasoning, I finally got Nathan to put on a simple white T-shirt and jeans that had just come out of the wash the day before. He left all of his Christmas gifts and all of his new clothes and stepped onto the plane without any bags.

Just Nathan.

And something about that episode drove home a realization to both Nathan and me. Nathan could mature as a man. He could grow stronger in many areas over time. But the OCD, the ADHD, the other issues were never going to go away. There would be no magic bullet to heal him. Yes, a miraculous healing was possible, or someday there might be a cure for some of his issues. But our present reality was to accept the limitations of his life and move forward as sustainably as we could. The letters that described his limitations would probably be with him—and with me—for the rest of our lives.

....

Imagination helped me adjust my expectations as a mama who had wanted life for my children to be perfect. We would never compare a zebra to a Dalmatian and judge it as less than perfect because it had stripes instead of spots. A butterfly should not be judged as weak because its wings are not as tough as a buffalo's hide. And a sick or wounded zebra or butterfly should not be expected to run or fly the same way a healthy one would.

We are all complex people, each with areas of strength and areas in which we are fragile or broken. In a fallen world, imperfections will attend our days until we move into eternity. And we must learn to make allowances for those broken areas while holding ourselves and others accountable for doing the best we can with what we have—and realizing that none of our flaws and broken places can change our inherent value as persons.

I had to learn that God never intended me to judge my children's value by how well they fit the assembly line of cultural expectations or my own dreams of what I thought motherhood should be like.

Each of them was an individual, one-of-a-kind design. Each had a special purpose in the world. And each had a special set of gifts and challenges that affected the way they operated in the world.

God had ordained that I would be the mama of these unique children, tasked with shepherding them through life and teaching them what unconditional love meant. It was my stewardship to parent my sweet little ones with all the faith and joy I had chosen as my foundation for the other areas in my life.

....

So often, through many years of hosting mom conferences, writing books, and speaking all over the world, I have told stories about my children. And I've always included tales about my children's mistakes and downfalls as well as sweet stories lived in our home. I've also been honest about my own depression and feelings of failure. But because I am oriented to living a life of joy and celebrating beauty, I've always tended to focus more on the ideals by which our family sought to live rather than the hardships of our everyday life. As a result, people have often made comments like, "Raising children must have just been easier for you than it was for me. They must be naturally mature children, ready to obey you, natural learners."

Let me say it now: Nothing about raising my children was easy. Much of it was joyful. Some of it was fun. All of it was meaningful. But easy? No. In fact, as I have related in this book, many dark, challenging days filled my journey of motherhood. Yet my foundational faith told me every day that God was good and that He had given me this day to live out my faith in Him by doing my best to bring light, goodness, and kindness into the world. And so it was amidst my struggles and trials that I learned the secret of celebrating life as it had been given to me.

Nathan and my other different children taught me a lot about that. If I had not been given them to love, I might never have learned that it's possible to be content even when life feels out of control. That as long as we assume we cannot be happy until we can control all the circumstances of our lives, we will continue to be unhappy. That freedom can be found in surrendering to God's transcendent purposes, which are infinitely greater than our finite understanding.

Accepting the limitations of mental illness, the limitations of life in general, was an essential step for my learning to make peace with life as it is, as it comes to me every day. Allowing God to unfold my fingers one at a time from my tightly held expectations for order and fulfillment led to an ability to celebrate each day for whatever it brought. It gave me an understanding that the divine love of God filled each moment, His companionship attended to me through each trial, and His care would cover every concern.

Still, on a daily basis, I have to remember to release, to choose patience, to ask for forgiveness when I blow it. But now we have a rhythm to our family that is built on a foundation of unconditional love. No matter what happens, at the end of the day, this is the place where we all return:

- "I am committed to loving you and accepting you as God has made you."
- "I will always be here for you."
- "I will always have your back and be a friend, whatever life holds."
- "I will help you search for answers and support your growth."
- "I will be a refuge you can come home to."
- "We are a family, and we will love each other always and always."

....

I can honestly say that loving Nathan was one of the best gifts I have ever received from God. In him I saw breathtaking beauty in forms I could never have imagined. Experiencing his loudness afresh helped me to appreciate his intense passion for life. Understanding his teasing antics as part of his exuberant engagement with life gave me more patience to affirm who he was at each stage.

On top of that, learning to really see Nathan—his heart, his possibilities, his precious worth to God—has helped me see others as well. Loving him has widened the parameters of my heart and taught me to look beyond external appearances and understand hearts. And this in turn has led me on pathways of deeper love and heartfelt compassion for others.

I will admit that, even now, my feelings do not always match my understanding in these areas. Especially when I am busy or exhausted, I do not always feel like affirming Nathan (or my other children), meeting his incessant needs, making allowances for his issues, or finding ways to relate to him. Sometimes I want him to stop having needs or opinions, just for twenty-four hours.

But by faith I'm usually able to accept his issues and choose to behave in a loving way, knowing that I am investing in his life—my heart validating his heart's cry for acceptance. This is the way of love—laying down our lives, choosing to invest in others as a habit of life, and expressing their value and our commitment even if our feelings are not always exactly matching.

And when I put away all the cultural expectations, all my selfish desires that life should be the way I planned it to be, Nathan is there before me as my beloved, cherished son, my friend, my child of delight and mirth. This process has indeed been a journey for me—one step at a time toward maturity—but I have learned so much, and the reward has been great.

On top of that, my respect for Nathan as a man and my admiration of him as a writer continue to increase every year. His insight into people, his love for life, and his deep understanding of what is precious in life enrich me every time we talk. His loyalty and love help us maintain a "best friend" relationship.

I go to Nathan for encouragement when I am down and need understanding. Deeply wounding relationships and profoundly painful circumstances have drawn the two of us together in seasons where we talked on the phone for at least an hour a day. I sorely miss my "Nathan time" when either of us is away on a trip and can't connect daily.

Does this mean that I have conquered all my selfish desire that Nathan, Clay, and the rest of my children will make my life easier? Of course not. I struggle most days with wanting to get a better handle on our lives. And I would love to have just one year that was free of conflict and trouble—or maybe just a month? Or perhaps a week?

Even after many years of being stretched and leaning in to God to gain insight, I still find I am deeply flawed. And I still find myself surprised at ways that I offend Nathan's OCD sensibilities. Even as an adult, he is somewhat of a mystery to me.

These days, however, I seek to understand more than to judge. Nathan has given me this gift. My whole imperfect, exasperating family has given me this gift.

Accepting reality and deciding to love our unique puzzle

brings a freedom and sense of peace that can come only from surrendering to the life that we have been given.

My heart will always break anew when I remember the moment when I found my precious son sitting broken on the basement stairs—grown into manhood and yet for the moment unable to deal with his life. The feelings of helplessness are still very real. These memories have not faded. There is always a part of me that fears for him having to endure other such moments as he moves through his life. Yet I move ahead, by faith, hoping that the heartbreaks will be fewer, the happy times more frequent, and that there will always be someone who sees and loves the amazing man God has created my Nathan to be, inside and out.

CHAPTER 13

Watch Me Fly!

....

Living for God's Applause

NATHAN

I had always been told that being different was a good thing. Countless people and TV shows repeated that message. But somewhere along the way I began to feel that maybe my brand of different didn't quite fit into the kind of "uniqueness" they were talking about.

My different was *too* different from the normal kind of different.

I can still remember sitting in yet another counselor's office sometime after my OCD diagnosis. My mom sat next to me, talking to a young woman who looked no more than fifteen years older than I was. Her name was Carrie. She was a therapist who specialized in cases like mine. And she was getting ready to "help" me.

I turned to look outside the window next to me while they talked. From the fifth floor I watched an oak tree's red leaves as they shook gently in the breeze that autumn had softly ridden in on.

Below I could see cars pulling in and out of parking spaces. A handsome, well-dressed, fortysomething man climbed into a silver BMW and drove off. I wondered why he was there. I wondered why *I* was there. I wondered if even men in suits and nice cars felt "not normal" sometimes.

Suddenly I realized that both my mom and the counselor had stopped talking and were looking at me.

"Isn't that right, Nathan?" my mom said softly, in an encouraging tone.

"I'm sorry. What?" I tried frantically to remember anything that had been said in the past five minutes.

My ADHD had taken my mind on a brief intermission, and for the past five minutes I had been driving my own silver sports car down a distant highway in my mind, leaving this office in the dust.

I snapped back into the real world as my mom was walking out the door, leaving me alone with the counselor so the session could begin. My fingers felt the ribbed cloth of the chair as I put my sweaty hands beneath my legs.

Carrie looked me in the eye. I held her gaze shortly before looking away awkwardly. She was pretty, and her face held a uniquely caring expression. I didn't really know where to look, so I stared at the floor. I felt lonely and exposed. But as her gentle voice reached out to the awkward teenage boy in front of her, I felt a gentle sense of safety fall over me.

I looked up at her and then around the room. Lining the walls were medical books that in some weird way assured me that I was finally in a place where no matter what I said, for once it wouldn't be surprising or shocking. It would simply be another day at the office.

Carrie asked me questions about my life, my friends, the girls I liked, my family, what kind of things I liked to do, and what kind of things made me anxious. I wasn't usually very inclined to open up to strangers, but her eyes held genuine warmth and interest, and I began to like her.

After twenty minutes of talking, she began to ask me more weighted questions. She asked if my mind was ever like a TV that never stopped changing channels. It was. In fact, my mind had changed channels fifteen times in just the small amount of time I had been in her office. She asked me what kinds of things I felt compelled to do. I told her about my hand washing, my shower rituals, and how when I felt dirty I worried that I would permanently contaminate the people, places, and memories I loved the most.

As we talked, I found the words gently forced out of my mouth. But I wondered what she thought as she looked at a junior in high school talking about his fear of touching people or his compulsion to wipe his hands every few seconds. Did she think I was crazy? Or was she used to this—seeing people every day who struggled with issues like mine?

While the session was surprisingly cathartic, it also left me feeling suddenly alone. I had the vague sense that all my life, unbeknownst to me, I had been listening and singing along to a song that no one else could hear, and try as I might, I simply couldn't hit the Off button.

I would eventually learn that my song was beautiful.

But it didn't feel that way on the afternoon when I realized I wasn't normal and might never be.

....

So it turned out that I wasn't normal. But in the years following my discovery of these things, I would routinely and consistently forget, only to be reminded abruptly and without warning of how flawed and different I really am.

There was that time in New York when I had begun to think of myself as the holy Christian kid being a light to the dark world of acting school. Then came the night at a party when I did something very stupid and non-youth-group-appropriate that somehow ended up on Facebook for all the world to see. A sibling wrote to express both love and disappointment in me. And when I read that letter, I hit square one with a thud.

Even worse was the time I've already described, when I felt like I was finally fitting in and becoming a normal guy at twenty-one, only to succumb to an OCD attack and almost miss my flight back to Los Angeles. That's the one that left me sitting on my basement stairs with my head in my hands, wondering what my new friends would think if they saw me broken and crying like a little kid because I felt too dirty to move.

It hurts, having your humanity thrown in your face time and again. I think it's something each of us experiences to different degrees. For one reason or another, we will all feel the sting of humiliation that comes from being broken humans living in a broken place, trying to fix the world with broken tools.

Prolonged exposure to this thing called life can cause a plethora of side effects, including bitterness, insecurities, the feeling that we might end up alone, pushing people away, and the fear that if there is a God, He could never love, much less use, someone as broken, weird, and unable to get it right as we are.

Which leaves us asking the question, "What now?"

....

The sun had been hot when I arrived at the Gaylord Palms Hotel in Kissimmee, Florida. But it was cold backstage as I waited to perform in the grand ballroom. The muffled sounds of acts preceding mine served as a countdown to my turn.

For the past week a talent competition had been going on. Thousands of young hopefuls had gathered to be paraded in front of top Hollywood agents and producers, hoping for a chance to live the dream of being discovered.

My parents had sent me here as a sign of support after I gave them the heart-attack-inducing news that I'd decided to become an actor/singer-songwriter/writer instead of going to college. After a week of competing with the other young artists, I had somehow made it to the final talent showcase. I would be performing an original song alongside a few select actors, comedians, dancers, vocalists, and other singer-songwriters.

I heard the roar of nearly a thousand people as an amazingly talented vocalist walked offstage. Shivers went down my spine, and I felt my palms begin to sweat. I looked around the backstage waiting room. On my right was a professional dancer, warming up by bending in ways that hurt me just to watch. To my left was a guitarist in a brightly colored shirt, rehearsing scales at a speed that I had previously thought impossible—guaranteed to wow the crowd.

Suddenly I felt completely out of place. I was surrounded by the best of the best, artists who had spent years becoming masters at their craft, each of them dressed to the nines and clearly capable of winning the competition. And there I was in the middle of them, the kid in ripped jeans and a plain white T-shirt who barely knew how to play the piano because I could never focus during my lessons, who had just learned a few chords so I could write a song.

I grew increasingly nervous as I waited. Then I heard my name for the five-minute warning. I slowly walked to the wing of the stage, knowing soon it would be my turn to have all those eyes expectantly on me. A dancer came offstage after giving a performance that received a standing ovation.

GOD IS OUT THERE IN THE DARK RIGHT PAST
THE SPOTLIGHT, WATCHING ME PERFORM
THIS SONG CALLED LIFE. I DON'T THINK HE'S
WAITING FOR MISTAKES OR COUNTING
THE MESS-UPS. I THINK HE'S WAITING
TO JUMP TO HIS FEET IN APPLAUSE.

"Awesome job," I said as she walked toward me out of breath. "That was amazing."

Her smile was brilliant but humble. "Thanks, but you guys are the amazing ones, writing songs that bare your heart. You're the ones with talent!"

Then I heard it, the voice that seemed to boom across the ballroom and echo in my empty stomach.

"Please welcome Nathan Clarkson!"

My heart started beating at marathon speed. I told my feet it was time, and reluctantly they carried me around the corner and into the harsh eye of the spotlight.

The sound of polite clapping died into an eerie silence as I walked to the piano, pulled back the bench, and sat down. I could feel the breathing expectation in the air as my fingers touched the keys of the baby grand. There I sat, unqualified, unskilled, underdressed, and under the speculation of nearly a thousand pairs of eyes.

It comforted me to know that somewhere in the dark of the room, past the shine of the lights, my mom was out there. But that comfort was quickly drowned out by the fear of messing up in front of all the important people.

I shut my eyes hard.

Then . . . I started.

My hands began to play what I had practiced. I hoped they remembered where they were supposed go because I was feeling a little numb. But for those three minutes I tried to forget about the judging eyes in the room, forget how out of place I was, forget the talent I lacked, and just play the song that I was here to play.

So I did.

The song was called "Watch Me Fall."[9] And I did fall a few times while I performed it. Several times my fingers hit the wrong keys, and I lost the tempo more than once. But I kept on playing. With all my heart I sang out the words I had written and pounded away on this instrument until there were no more notes to play.

Finally I sat there with the last note of the song still ringing in the room. I knew I had made mistakes, but I had made it through. Now I waited, head down, eyes still shut.

Silence.

And then, amazingly, applause. Deafening applause.

I carefully opened my eyes to see the entire crowd on their feet.

After the show was done, I walked into the lobby with congratulating hands patting me on the back as I made my way slowly through the crowd toward my mom, who ran up to embrace me.

She said nothing about the mistakes, but simply hugged me and said, "I'm so proud of you. You were amazing! I love you so much."

....

I think God is out there in the dark right past the spotlight, watching me perform this song called life. He knows I'm underqualified, scared, not good enough, not even normal.

But I don't think He's waiting for mistakes or counting the mess-ups. I think He's a Parent waiting to jump to His feet in applause. And when it's all done, when I'm finally walking toward Him, I don't think He is even going to remember the keys I missed or the mistakes I made.

Instead I think He is going run to embrace me and say, "I'm so proud of you. You were amazing! I love you so much."

Sally

Sometimes I forget the moments, the days, the years of anguish, grief, frustration, helplessness, and exhaustion that went into raising Nathan. And then with one memory or a few words shared, it all comes back.

After Nathan graduated from high school, he tried to decide what he was going to do with his life. I wondered, too, and felt some fear and insecurity about how to direct him. College did not seem an appropriate prospect—academics were not his forte. For a while he worked with a landscaping company building garden walls and digging holes for planting trees. A job as a pizza delivery boy lasted about a week. Then one day, when we were sitting on our front porch talking, he said, "Mom, I think I am going to pursue becoming an actor in Hollywood."

Sure you are—not! I thought to myself. *You have never acted in your life, except for the role you played when you were six years old.* To me, this newly expressed ambition to be a professional entertainer sounded a little like a little boy wanting to quarterback a famous football team. *This is never going to happen*, I told myself.

Yet from the time Nathan was little, he had loved being in front of crowds at our conferences. When he was about seven, he'd given a never-to-be-forgotten speech about a war hero. And Nathan had loved performing his magic shows at birthday parties. So there were some ghosts of past years that pointed to a hidden talent not yet expressed.

Still skeptical but not wanting to discourage him, I said, "I understand your excitement. Tell me more, and I will pray about this."

He spoke of wanting to attend the New York Film Academy. And he continued to talk about this newly expressed dream. But nothing really came of the talk, and the dream was left on the shelf.

Almost a year later, a Christian acting and talent agency announced over the radio that it was holding auditions. *Just a moneymaking scam*, I thought. But seven of my friends called and said, "Nathan has been talking and praying about this for over a year. You should take him for an audition."

And so I took him to a hotel where he met with the agents and sang a song. They told him he was just the type of young man they were looking for and encouraged him to attend the national conference in Florida, where Hollywood agents, movie producers, and managers would be judging the winners.

We suspected this organization was just playing on the desires of innocent kids like Nathan, and we felt conflicted about his going forward with this group. We did not relish his being in an arena where he would probably lose and come home feeling more discouraged and disheartened than ever. Besides, the trip would cost quite a bit of money—with airplane flights, hotel, meals, and the conference itself.

But as I prayed, I thought, *If God has opened this door, how can you not walk through it with him in faith?*

I wanted Nathan to have something positive in his life because he had been floundering from this to that since he had graduated over a year before. I felt that we needed to take risks of faith to help Nathan find his footing in life. So I talked Clay into letting Nathan compete. We scratched together the money for Nathan and me to fly to Florida.

The competition would last five days. Children and young adults from all over the country would be participating, with almost a thousand people in attendance.

Fear of Nathan's failure amidst so many competitors clouded my emotions with darkness and dread. Nathan believed this was his big chance—but what chance did he really have? I knew his heart would be broken if he didn't have the opportunity to move ahead in this field he was so passionate about.

Every day he would pray fervently with me and beg God to "open a door for me so that I can find a way to get into the acting arena to tell my stories." His young, untested faith was strong. In light of so many disappointments in his life, I prayed a little more desperately, pleading with God that He would do a miracle for him.

I did believe God had something ahead for my wonderful

Nathan. But the years had been so hard on both of us that I had a hard time believing for him. I prayed as sincerely as I could. I just wasn't sure this outcome would be any different from all the other times in his life when he had given his all, only to find out that some of his limitations held him back.

But God had prompted me to find the money for the conference and competition. So I put aside my own plans so I could go to Florida with him for a week. Nathan had big dreams, and he needed his mama to be a companion in what he believed God could do—a miracle!

Once we arrived in Florida, Nathan practiced his original song over and over on any free piano he could find—in the lobby, in empty conference rooms. He would sing out with all of his heart and bang the piano with his whole force. (He had never learned how to read music. The piece consisted of lots of chords behind the words and melody he had created.)

While he practiced, I would retreat to my sterile, lonely hotel room, fall to my knees on the rough industrial carpet, and beg God for mercy, for compassion, for supernatural help for Nathan to do his best. Sincere, deeply felt pleas flowed again and again from my heart to His Father heart.

"Please, God, out of Your generous love and compassion, give Nathan blessing and favor as only You can, and help him have a place to flourish this week. Give him hope and a way forward."

Picking myself and my heart off the floor, I would then seek out Nathan again. And again I would become his best friend, his most enthusiastic cheerleader, and his adoring fan.

"Go out there and sparkle to the last row of the auditorium," I whispered in his ear when it was time for him to go backstage and for me to find my seat in the audience. "You are pure sunshine."

At the announcement of his name, Nathan walked confidently to the grand piano. (His extroverted Superman complex has always served him well when it comes to performing.) He sat on the bench, took a deep breath, looked down at his hands, and breathed out a sigh. Then he began pounding out the same chords he had practiced so faithfully all week.

Nervous anxiety flew through the recesses of my heart, not because I cared that much about his performance, but because I so wanted him to have an emotional win on this night, his grand debut.

Sparkle did come from his eyes, fervency from his voice, confidence and strength from his spirit as he played and sang. A hush fell at the end of his piece. My heart beat so wildly I was sure it could be heard in the room.

Then suddenly the whole room was standing, clapping, whistling, cheering. I was crying, smiling, laughing, yelling with the crowd. And my amazing Nathan just smiled and bowed as if he had expected it all along.

This memory still brings deep, grateful tears to me today, almost ten years later.

But surprises were still in store for us. A silver-haired man, elegantly dressed in formal attire for the auspicious occasion of the evening, stepped up to the microphone. He cleared his voice as a hint that the audience was to be still.

"After observing hundreds of talented young men and women this weekend, I have come to the conclusion that several performers in the crowd deserve to be awarded a ten-thousand-dollar scholarship to the New York Film Academy to further their training."

We clapped politely as he announced the first few winners.

Then he said, "Nathan Clarkson, will you come forward? I have rarely seen such passion in a young man, and I think you have a promising future in our industry. So I would like to extend a scholarship to you."

My jaw literally fell open as Nathan turned to me. "See, Mama," he said, "God still does miracles."

This award led to Nathan's year of studying acting in New York City, the move to Los Angeles, and eventually to the production of Nathan's first movie, *Confessions of a Prodigal Son*, which is yet another story of God's faithfulness. (Look for it on Netflix!)

I am so proud of what Nathan has achieved in his life—and what I believe he will continue to achieve. I can't wait to hear the stories he will tell, to see the light he will bring to a world and an industry often shrouded in darkness. I know his passion, his perseverance. I am absolutely convinced that whatever crazy twists and turns his life takes, he will find a way to tell stories that need to be told. (Who knows? Maybe his hero stories will be the ones that capture the imagination of some other little boy who struggles with being different and needs a dream to aspire to.)

I am even prouder of the man Nathan has become along the way. All those years of challenge and difficulty, being labeled as "disruptive" and "too much" created in Nathan a compassionate heart and a humble dependence on God. I am convinced that the stories he is now telling could never have had such depth if his soul had not been shaped by the pain and tears of being different.

As for me as Nathan's mama—I have to admit I am proud of me, too. I have never been the perfect mama. I am flawed, selfish, often distracted, sometimes too idealistic for my own good. But I, too, persevered in letting a different, sometimes tortured little boy know that he was loved unconditionally, that he was listened to, that he had a safe place to be himself and the potential to take on a hero's role in his own life. And most important, that he was a completely beloved, completely accepted child of his heavenly Father, who made him on purpose and had work for him to do in the world.

Life with my outside-the-box boy has been more difficult than I ever dreamed—and more rewarding than I ever thought possible. And it has been filled with treasures that I am quite sure my heavenly Father knew I would not discover on any other path. God has used Nathan and his differences to teach me more about His ways than any other relationship or circumstance has. Through this son of mine, I learned that our heavenly Father brings miracles of redemption and promise to each of us when we fully live into the puzzle of who we are and who we were meant to be.

Even with all the twists and turns of our "different"

journey, all the mysteries we may never fully understand, Nathan has always been a gift of love to me. Not only did I gain new treasures of faith and understanding, but I acquired a deeply valued best friend for life.

To me, he'll always be Superman.

EPILOGUE

Don't Give Up on Your Story

NATHAN

I turned the pages slowly, making sure not to miss one inch of the pictures before me. I was seven years old, and while I still struggled with reading, the tale splayed open on my lap told its story through so much more than words.

The expertly painted pictures printed across the glossy pages told the story of a knight with blond hair and blue eyes like mine on his way to do battle with an unseen dragon. On his chest he wore thick and shiny armor, and in his hand he held his sword. He was confident and ready as he looked out over the fields, ready to face his unseen foe.

I turned the page once more, and I drew in my breath as the dragon appeared and reared its ugly head. The great serpent walked into the story towering above our hero, flashing his scaly skin for all to see. He breathed fire into the air, creating black clouds of smoke over the knight.

The knight looked at his foe with determination, no doubt trying his best to keep his fear at bay. The artist had so vividly painted the confrontation between the minuscule knight and the epically proportioned dragon that I wondered how the tiny warrior had any chance at all.

On the next page, the pair met in a glorious collision, the dragon ferociously clawing at our hero while the knight swung his sword mightily.

The battle raged on as the pages turned beneath my little hands. Another page turn, and the dragon was clawing through the knight's armor, tearing it like paper and knocking our hero to the ground. I drew in my breath as I turned the page again, hoping and praying that the battle wasn't over.

It wasn't.

As the next picture appeared, I saw the knight, beaten and broken, find his feet once more. Determination tightened his face as he lifted his sword and, with one final cry and swing of his weapon, slew his foe.

As my wide eyes took in the spectacle of the grand tale, I felt in my heart a longing to be as mighty and brave as the hero fighting a dragon. I was only seven, but I was already letting the story sink into my own narrative.

I look back now and think about how as a young boy I was drawn to the stories of heroes (and superheroes!) taking on epic foes that stood with daunting presence, poised to carry out their evil plans. The odds were almost always overwhelming. The enemies seemed far bigger, far more powerful, and often were greater in number. But the heroes remained steadfast, sure of their mission, resolute in defeating their foes—even when they had fallen, their armor cracked, and all hope seemed lost.

Something in my seven-year-old heart knew these stories were important. And the more I immersed myself in them, the more I came to see my life in the context of a story. I began to see the choices I made as important to the tale I was weaving. I may not have been going up against real dragons, but now I saw my everyday struggles as the battles I had been given to fight. And the choices I made in the context of these battles were the elements that would make my story one worth telling or not.

In my soul I knew I wanted to be the hero of the story I was in. But so often, like the knight in my picture book, I felt tiny in comparison to the looming dragons of anxiety, learning disabilities, obsessions, and self-doubt. So often I wondered how I could ever win. But still I marched to battle, trusting that in the end the heroes always win, even if they're beaten, tired, and worn. That while the battle is hard, good will always defeat evil and light will always win out over dark.

We all have dragons in our lives. They may not be quite so obvious as a towering, scaly monster, but still we feel their ominous presence as they hover above us, threatening our dreams, our loves, our very lives. And we all have the choice of giving in to the darkness we face, letting the dragons lay waste to everything we care about. But we can also choose to be the heroes of our stories—standing firm, staying strong, and getting up even when we are knocked over, wounded, discouraged.

At some point, no matter what we choose, we will undoubtedly feel the sting of claws ripping through our armor, the panic of our breath growing short, the weariness of our wills wearing thin. But I believe with all my heart that should we continue to fight, continue to choose the way of the hero, we will eventually see victory.

So we need to ask ourselves: *What are the dragons in my life? What is the battle I have been given to fight?*

And then comes the big question, the decision that makes the difference:

What kind of story do I want to tell?

"WHAT IS THE BATTLE
I HAVE BEEN GIVEN
TO FIGHT?"

TO CONTINUE THE CONVERSATION
WITH SALLY AND NATHAN, VISIT
THEDIFFERENTBOOK.COM
OR E-MAIL THEM AT
ADMIN@WHOLEHEART.ORG.